SUPER BRAIN POWER

6 KEYS TO UNLOCKING YOUR HIDDEN GENIUS

SUPER BRAIN POWER

6 KEYS TO UNLOCKING YOUR HIDDEN GENIUS

JEAN MARIE STINE

PRENTICE HALL
Paramus, New Jersey 07652

Library of Congress Cataloging-in-Publication Data

Stine, Jean.
    Super brain power : 6 keys to unlocking your hidden genius / Jean Marie
      Stine.   p. cm.
    Includes bibliographical references and index.
    ISBN 0–13-013911–4   ISBN 0–7352-0133–1 (pbk.)
      1. Intellect—Problems, exercises, etc.   2. Multiple intelligences.
    I. Title.
    BF431.3.S75 2000
    153—dc21

                                                  00–060627

© 2000 by Jean Marie Stine

Acquisitions Editor: *Gloria Fuzia*
Production Editor: *Eve Mossman*
Interior Design/Layout: *Dee Coroneos*

Printed in the United States of America

10 9 8 7 6 5 4 3 2

ISBN 0-13-013911-4

PRENTICE HALL
Paramus, NJ 07652

On the World Wide Web at http://www.phdirect.com

Dianne Charlotte Wickes

If blood be the price of admiralty,
Lord God, you have paid it in full.
(with apologies to Rudyard Kipling)

Adieu, mon amour . . .

ABOUT THE AUTHOR

Jean Marie Stine has presented seminars on brain power, speed learning, and business writing throughout the United States.

She has worked with many of the leading human-potential and peak-performance consultants, including Jean Houston, Ken Wilber, Charles Garfield, Betty Edwards, Timothy Leary, Marianne Williams, Marilyn Ferguson, Richard Berne, Robin Norwood, and David Kreutzer.

She is the author or coauthor of more than two dozen nonfiction books, including *Double Your Brain Power* (Prentice-Hall, 1997), a selection of the Quality Paperback Bookclub and the One Spirit Bookclub; *It's All in Your Head: Amazing Facts About the Human Mind* (Macmillan, 1994); *Writing Successful Self-Help/How-To Books* (Wiley, 1996); and *The Best Guide to Motivation* (Renaissance, 2001).

Her novel, *Season of the Witch*, was recently filmed as *Synapse*, starring Karen Duffy. She currently resides in western Massachusetts, where she works with a number of civil-rights and gender-advocacy organizations.

ACKNOWLEDGMENTS

No author is honest who claims her book is possible without "a little help from my friends." This book was written and finished only through the love and support of Brenda Burke, Gary McKnight, Rachel Neulander, Norm B. (the only performer I know who reads the Romans as if they were living poets), and Piettit Desveaux.

The Haymarket for (when they're on it) the greatest mocha in the world, and Jake's for the only eggs Benedict worth standing in line on a New England winter Sunday morning. And, the crew at Kathy's Diner, who kept me fed the other six mornings of the week.

A big bouquet is also due to:

Polly Marie Hoffman (my mother), Adrienne Martinez-Barnes, and Richard F.X. O'Connor, all three for moral support along the way.

The best agent a girl could have, Bert Holtje, whose hairs are gray, only because of authors like me.

My patient editors at Prentice-Hall, Douglas Corcoran and Gloria Fuzia.

Finally, my housemate, inspiration, and partner, Frankie Hill, without whom . . .

CONTENTS

Days 1–4: The First Key
UNLOCKING YOUR VERBAL GENIUS

WHAT'S YOUR VERBAL IQ?   29

Days 5–7: The Second Key
UNLOCKING YOUR VISUAL GENIUS

WHAT'S YOUR VISUAL IQ?   71

Days 8–11: The Third Key
UNLOCKING YOUR LOGICAL GENIUS

WHAT'S YOUR LOGICAL IQ?   105

Days 12–14: The Fourth Key
UNLOCKING YOUR CREATIVE GENIUS

WHAT'S YOUR CREATIVE IQ?   143

Days 15–17: The Fifth Key
UNLOCKING YOUR PHYSICAL GENIUS

WHAT'S YOUR PHYSICAL IQ?   175

Days 18–21: The Sixth Key
UNLOCKING YOUR EMOTIONAL GENIUS

WHAT'S YOUR EMOTIONAL IQ?   207

PREFACE

Have you ever struggled to memorize a list of complicated names, dates, and rules for a forthcoming exam, or felt at a loss when unexpectedly called upon to provide the solution to a difficult problem during a company or group meeting? Have you ever been in the midst of a discussion and suddenly found yourself stumped about what to say next to get your point across?

Have you ever puzzled over a problem for hours or weeks without a clue and later realized the solution was right before your eyes all the time?

Have you ever been fooled by deceptive advertising, or been misled by a corporate prospectus, or overlooked an important flaw in your own or someone else's position—and ended up feeling sorry for it later?

Have you ever longed for a creative way to tell someone you love them, needed a world-class inspiration to save a tottering business, or been challenged to come up with a new theme for the parish fundraising campaign?

Have you ever struggled to learn how to repair a drainpipe, master a tennis stroke, give a permanent wave, or work with an unfamiliar keyboard configuration?

Have you ever had an abrasive relative you just couldn't find a way to deal with, or been unable to figure out why you failed to "click" at an important job interview, or failed to see what was preventing you from welding a promising group of people into a team that realizes its potential?

Of course you have. Everyone has.

Even Albert Einstein, possibly the supreme genius of the twentieth century, wished he were smarter when he found the math underlying his Unified Field Theory, intended to explain and unify all physics, was wrong.

HOW THIS BOOK CAN MAKE YOU SMARTER

We all yearn to be smarter, because we know in our hearts how important it is to every possible type of personal and professional fulfillment. "The secret of success," agrees Thomas Finley, a management consultant and author, isn't "personality, heredity, or education." All these "are a part of it, of course," he concedes. But Finley also notes that "there is something more important than any of them: the ability to think. The person who is truly able to learn, to reason, to remember is the absolute master of his or her own life. Leaders in every field, from skilled labor to nuclear research, have this one ability in common: They are able to think with greater speed, accuracy, and simple horse sense than those around them. In the last analysis, it is mental skill that pays off on most jobs."

Once expanding your brain power—and achieving the kind of genius that would carry you through the kinds of challenges described in the previous paragraph—was a dream. Scientific studies showed people typically drew on 10 percent or less of the brain's resources, even when thinking their hardest. Individuals seemed pretty much stuck with whatever level of intelligence they had achieved by the time they were old enough to take IQ tests. But scientists did not know why, or how people could gain access to the other 90 percent or so of their brain power.

Now a unique scientific breakthrough makes it possible for anyone to access the hidden genius of the remaining nine tenths of their brain power. If you want to, you can begin to take immediate advantage of this breakthrough by turning to the first day's exercise and following the easy, step-by-step instructions you'll find there. Then, do the same on each of the other twenty days of the program. Twenty-one days, a mere three weeks from now, this program will have expanded your intelligence so far that you will score higher by every measure of intelligence.

The super brain power program is a unique combination of leading-edge science, practical information, and easy-to-use techniques for enhancing performance and personal effectiveness while reducing the negative impact of stress. It can help anyone benefit from the hidden 90 percent of their genius. Though it is based on solidly established scientific research, this book presents a minimum of scientific terminology and esoteric theory. Instead, you will find a practical program built around concrete exercises that build vital success skills by unlocking mental abilities and capacities you already possess.

WHY THIS PROGRAM CAN DO WHAT IT CLAIMS

Over the years, various books and programs purported to show readers how to break through that 10 percent ceiling to draw on more of their brain power. But, as scientists had no clear understanding of why we were limited to such a tiny fraction of our mental capacities, no one could truly deliver on that promise.

The best all these publications and systems could offer was a few mental shortcuts for solving problems more quickly, or concentrating to pick up more detail, or recalling names, facts, and figures. Those who benefited from these programs did so not because of any actual increase in mental power, performance, or speed, but because they were using mental shortcuts that allowed them to make more efficient use of the one tenth of the brain they were already using. Otherwise, these programs did nothing to help people draw from the vast mental treasure of that untapped 90 percent.

Science has since learned that such programs were unsuccessful in augmenting mental performance because they were "looking where the light is." They based their assumptions on the thinking that there is only one kind of intelligence—logical problem solving, or occasionally two, if creativity were counted. However, as a result of research by Harvard's Howard Gardner, Ph.D., and others, we now know that there are six types of intelligence, not just one or two. We also know that each human being has been endowed with an equal measure of all six. And, according to Gardner, it is these six intelligences that hold the key to unlocking your hidden genius.

These six are verbal intelligence, visual intelligence, logical intelligence, creative intelligence, physical intelligence, and emotional intelligence. Everyone has known people who are good with words, or a real "brain," or super creative, or great with his or her hands, or who was a "born" leader. Now, it's possible to understand why. If you look back at the six paragraphs that opened this Preface, you will find each of these six intelligences represented in the examples given there.

Super Brain Power is the first book to provide practical techniques for achieving mental peak performance based on this new discovery. Expanding access to even one or two of these intelligences is enough to lift your brain power to the genius level, effectively doubling your intelligence. Maximizing all six will place you in the super-genius category. This book will lead you through a tested, comprehensive program designed to accomplish precisely that. In short, you no longer need to be a genius to unlock your hidden genius!

Most people make so little use of their mental capacities that to become outstanding in any walk of life—education, business, politics, health care—*all it takes is to optimize any one of your six intelligences!* A person can be a genius when it comes to cinematography (visual intelligence) without possessing an ounce of common sense (logical intelligence); someone can be a champion athlete (physical intelligence) and helpless when it comes to expressing him or herself (verbal intelligence); it's possible to be an award-winning advertising executive (creative intelligence) and wholly unable to get along harmoniously with others (interpersonal intelligence).

The same is true for you. Whatever your personal objective or challenge—whether it's making a convincing presentation, better communication with your spouse, getting that raise, superior athletic performance, owning your own business, better inventory control, dealing with a subordinate who is an excellent worker but can't get along with her or his colleagues, generating customer traffic, developing a new course curriculum—making better use of only one or two of your six intelligences is enough to move you to the genius class and carry you through to success.

Previous books about your six intelligences have approached the problem piecemeal, each centered around techniques for raising a single intelligence, again leaving the larger portion of our mental potential untapped. But this book will show you how to optimize not one or two, but all six intelligences, literally unlocking all 100 percent of your brain power. When you have completed the brain-friendly program showcased in the chapters that follow, you will find that with the other 90 percent of the brain at your command, you can achieve your goals, whatever they may be, and best any hurdles you encounter along the way.

HOW THIS BOOK IS ORGANIZED

This book opens with a brief overview that explains multiple intelligences and how they hold the key to extraordinary personal achievement. Titled "Success, the Six Intelligences and You," this overview describes each intelligence, people who have become famous using it, professions where it is a must, a few of the many skills you acquire when you begin exercising it, and the role that intelligence plays in realizing our deepest aspirations.

This overview section concludes with six mini-exercises. None takes more than a few minutes, and each will provide a boost to one of your key intelligences. I believe you will experience such immediate and powerful benefits that simply sampling one or two (you are encouraged to try all six) will be enough to motivate you to begin— and finish—this amazing three-week, twenty-one day program.

The remainder of the book presents the super brain power program itself: twenty-one mind-stretching techniques, organized into three- or four-day sections, each given focusing on a single intelligence.

Exercises/days 1–4:	Verbal intelligence
Exercises/days 5–7:	Visual intelligence
Exercises/days 8–11:	Logical intelligence
Exercises/days 12–14:	Creative intelligence
Exercises/days 15–17:	Physical intelligence
Exercises/days 18–21:	Emotional intelligence

Each portion of the program focused on a single intelligence begins with an interactive quiz that will help you estimate how high your IQ is in that particular intelligence. (You can recognize these quizzes easily, as they have titles such as, "What's Your Verbal IQ?" and "What's Your Visual IQ?"). These are followed by a brief introductory section explaining how you can unlock that intelligence and describing some of the amazing mental skills and abilities you acquire when you exercise it regularly. (You will find these sections immediately following the "What's your . . . IQ" quizzes, with titles such as "Unlocking Your Verbal Intelligence" and "Unlocking Your Visual Intelligence.")

Each day of the program presents one easy-to-follow, brain power-building exercise for developing a specific intelligence. Each provides detailed guidance that allows you to immediately begin putting the technique to use in your own life, and each is illustrated with a wealth of suggestions for practical everyday applications, plus inspiring stories drawn from my own clients, friends, and contemporary business headlines, describing how other people, just like you— some famous, some my clients, others personal friends—have applied it successfully to resolve critical issues and dilemmas they faced.

WHY THIS PROGRAM WON'T WORK IF YOU DON'T!

The super brain program is designed to take much of the work out of expanding your six intelligences. Each exercise has been constructed to be as easy to understand and use as possible. But, as with all exercise programs, the techniques this book presents won't do you a bit of good if you don't practice them and put a bit of effort into them. You won't get much benefit, either, if you see it as a chore, something you "have" to do, and attempt to slide through "by rote."

But, invest just thirty minutes per day for twenty-one days, perform each exercise faithfully, and at the end of three weeks, you will be astonished to discover just how much of your hidden genius you have unlocked. That's not too much to ask when the reward is super brain power, is it?

INTRODUCTION

SUCCESS, THE SIX INTELLIGENCES AND YOU

HOW THE SUPER BRAIN POWER PROGRAM CAN MAKE YOU 500 PERCENT SMARTER

This book contains a unique twenty-one-day program for "super-sizing" your brain power. These exercises and this program are rooted in a breakthrough scientific paradigm of intelligence and how we can maximize it. Dubbed the theory of "multiple intelligences," it has led to the discovery of brain power-boosting techniques that can profoundly enhance your likelihood of succeeding in every area of your life.

Converging investigations in neuroscience, creativity, perception, cognition, psychobiology, and developmental psychology reveal that everyone has not one, but six separate intelligences, each hardwired into a different region of the brain. Most people, due to background or heredity, grow up almost exclusively drawing on one of these six intelligences (and not even fully on that one) and are unaware of the existence of the others. I call these six intelligences your "hidden" genius.

This introductory section of the book will explain how the super brain power program can help you unlock this hidden genius. It will introduce you to some of the amazing abilities you will gain as you expand each of these intelligences. And it will conclude with six mini-exercises, one for each intelligence, so that you can test the power of this program before investing a single day in it.

UNLOCKING YOUR HIDDEN GENIUS

Most people whom we consider geniuses, people who have made their mark in the world, people such as Barbara Walters, Sam Walton, and Bill Gates, are generally individuals who, by some lucky accident, have succeeded in drawing on a second of the six intelligences or, in rare cases, a third. The rest of us plug along using one sixth, or more likely one tenth, of our total brain power.

But stick with the super brain power program and three weeks from today you will be drawing on all six intelligences, and you'll be well on the way to unlocking your hidden genius.

Super brain power is not just an empty promise, a pet theory of the author's, or a "trick" title designed to lure readers to this book. Instead, it is a practical system that anyone can benefit from, based on this new understanding about the human mind. When you have completed the step-by-step program presented in the pages that follow and have wholly developed all six intelligences, you will discover you possess all the skills you need to achieve your goals (whether those goals are becoming a CEO or a minister, returning to college, or buying a dream home by the sea) and overcome whatever obstacles lie in your path.

How You Can Make Yourself 500 Percent Smarter

Previously science saw "intelligence" as the part of the mind that engages in conscious thinking and problem solving—a single, monolithic mental phenomenon. The accepted view, in short, was that there was only one kind of intelligence and that, according to *The American Heritage Dictionary of the English Language*, was the "ability to form concepts, solve problems, obtain information, reason, and perform other intellectual operations."

As a result, most scientific research, the educational system, and efforts to raise intelligence focused on conscious, logical thinking. The other five intelligences remained unknown, unexplored, and, for the most part, undeveloped. Those of us who, due to some factor in our background or heredity, found it easy to use our logical intelligence thrived under this system and were singled out as "most likely to succeed." This led to the misconception that only a small number of us (one sixth or less) are smart, and the rest are doomed to tag along mentally behind.

As educational consultant Leslie Shelton of Project Read has written, "Teachers long noticed that IQ scores failed to measure and reflect all of the abilities of children. Why were kids who were good in math and science considered smart while those who were good athletes, artists or musicians simply talented? Perhaps we were not recognizing children's various talents fairly."

Unfortunately, those of us whose strengths lay in one of the other five intelligences struggled to adapt to materials and approaches focused solely on logical brain power. But without understanding and support for our own particular form of intelligence, we typically failed to do as well in school and in most forms of employment pretesting. Thus, we were judged less promising by teachers and employers. In consequence, we grew up believing we weren't as intelligent as other people and suffered from lowered self-esteem and a negative view of our capabilities.

Now, due to the efforts of Howard Gardner of the Harvard Graduate School and Boston University, we know there are more intelligences than one. Gardner first presented this view of intelligence to the general public in his book, *Frames of Mind: The Theory of Multiple Intelligences.* There he described the discovery of six separate, distinct intelligences, each with its own programming (learning), information processing (thinking/problem solving) and data storage (memory) systems. He also noted that, although each intelligence is autonomous, they can, and do, work in concert at times (usually at the level of the deep unconscious).

To bring things to the practical level, this means each of us has the equivalent of six separate brains, and all the mental power that implies, locked away inside us. But since we have been training only one of these forms of intelligence, the mind's true potential has barely been scratched, and the rest remains hidden from sight.

Like most scientific discoveries, when it's finally explained, the theory of multiple intelligences feels intuitively right (as if you've known it all along without being able to put it into words). For instance, while the ability to reason logically might at first blush seem to represent intelligence, it's a well-known fact that most scientific and mathematical advances occurred, not as the result of reasoning, but in flashes of insight.

And what about people with high IQs who just can't seem to get the knack of anything physical? And how about those whose IQs measure lower, but on whom the "geniuses" must rely to repair their plumbing and fix their cars?

Creative thinking, which runs a close second in most people's minds to logical problem solving as a valid form of intelligence, is not quite the end all of intelligence, either. Many creative people are flat broke, and many "duller" intellects grow wealthy. And what about people whose genius appears to lie solely in making the best strategic use of the abilities of others? Or those who can just look at a problem and seem know the answer without thinking?

When you stop to think about intelligence this way, it becomes clear that the evidence of more kinds of intelligence than one was staring us in the face all along, and only the self-blinders of our own assumptions kept us from realizing it before.

The theory of "multiple" intelligence is so new that experts still argue over the precise number. However, all are agreed that the six that follow play key roles in our daily lives and key roles in determining our success or failure. These six are

- *Verbal intelligence*—encompasses the realm of words: speaking, writing, reading, even listening

- *Visual intelligence*—encompasses the realm of sight and seeing

- *Logical intelligence*—encompasses the realm of reason, consciously directed thinking, and certain aspects of problem solving

- *Creative intelligence*—encompasses the realm of originality, innovation, insight, and the generation of new ideas

- *Physical intelligence*—encompasses the realm of the body, coordination, dexterity, and the acquisition of physical skills

- *Emotional intelligence*—encompasses the realm of feeling, both one's own and those of others, including all inter- and intrapersonal relationships

Something like whether various key brain systems have their own intelligence may seem esoteric, far removed from such practicalities of daily life as meetings with coworkers, family squabbles, starting a business, or managing employees. But take a closer look at these six (verbal, visual, logical, creative, physical, emotional) and you will find all the fundamentals of living: communication, sight, reason, inspiration, the body, our relationships and our feelings.

What if you could raise your mental efficiency in all six of these arenas by just 10 percent? That means a total net gain in brain power of 60 percent! Now stretch your imagination and try to envision what your life would be like if you could unlock the mental reserves of all six of your intelligences. That would be a minimum 500 percent jump! Would you feel smart enough then? Would that improve your ability to manage a more fruitful family life, improve the quality of your work, fulfill your own personal dreams?

You can achieve all this because it's possible to boost each intelligence by exercising it constantly, just as you can exercise and strengthen muscles. In short, you can build your mental muscles, just as you can your physical muscles. A picture of yourself as a mental Sylvester Stallone, bulging with a muscular IQ, that's the promise of the discovery of multiple intelligences.

Three Ways This Program Unlocks Your Brain Power

The previous paradigm of intelligence wasn't just misleading to scientists. As noted earlier, the exclusive focus on conscious reasoning actually kept your true intelligence shackled. This single-minded approach sabotaged brain power on three different fronts:

1. *Only logical intelligence was developed and rewarded.* Every measure of intellectual potential from schools to the boardroom was based on an individual's expertise at consciously reasoning through problems. Desirability and promotability were determined by the degree of proficiency someone achieved with this faculty. No effort was devoted to any of the remaining five intelligences, leaving five sixths of the average person's brain power unused and unappreciated. Nor was someone's having tapped one of the other intelligences—physical or emotional intelligence, say—seen as enhancing his or her desirability as a student or employee.

2. *The other five intelligences were devalued and unexploited.* People who didn't prove instantly apt at conscious reasoning but had a strong knack for, say, creative or physical or emotional intelligence made little attempt to develop them. Instead, they continued struggling to expand their logical intelligence.

3. *Those who did not excel at this kind of thinking saw themselves as less able and intelligent than others.* Because they rated so low by standard measurements of intelligence, they labeled themselves "dumb," "stupid," "not very bright," "lacking in smarts." They had lower expectations for their own capabilities, were less likely to attempt to cope with serious challenge, and were less likely to have a positive outcome. As Gardner has noted, "entrepreneurs think my theory is great . . . they are people who weren't considered that smart in school because they didn't have good notation skills—you know, moving little symbols around. But they . . . often were understanding things that other people, including their teachers, weren't understanding."

The new understanding of the way the brain functions empowers you to put vast, untapped mental resources to action on your behalf. The discovery of multiple intelligences unlocks this hidden genius because you follow three steps.

1. *Train and value all your intelligences.* You no longer have to limit yourself to a mere sixth of your mental wattage. With access to all six intelligences, you can take off your mental "blinders" at last. In addition, rather than futilely attempting to apply one kind of intelligence to all six domains, you can apply the appropriate intelligence (or combination of intelligences) to whatever difficulties you encounter. Further, this paradigm has already led educators and managers to downplay the value of logical intelligence in their recruitment and promotional efforts, and to test for other intelligences as well.

2. *Make greater use of any intelligence you are already tapping.* Even if you have a knack for creativity, or possess unusual physical dexterity, or are in tune with the emotional realm, you probably weren't taught to get 100 percent from it. Applying what you know about multiple intelligences allows you to optimize gifts you already possess.

3. *Appreciate just how smart you really are.* If you are someone who has concluded you aren't very bright, merely because your current long suit doesn't encompass reasoned problem solving, then you will arrive at a revolutionary, positive picture of your own innate gifts. Understanding that your particular form of intelligence is just as valuable a tool for personal and career progress as logical intelligence can give you the confidence to tackle challenges that once would have seemed daunting and to accomplish things you once considered impossible.

Fourteen Proven Benefits of Developing the Six Intelligences

Studies by Howard Gardner, Patricia Phipps, David Lazear, and others have verified that those who unlock their six intelligences gain dozens of faculties that are vital to thriving in the fast-changing world of the twenty-first century. Not surprisingly, people who have gone out of their way to build these skills are more likely to describe themselves as leading fulfilling lives, having rewarding careers, and realizing their dreams.

Remember, you don't need any special talents to "super-size" your brain power like this. You already have genius locked away within you. It's your heritage; you were born with it. The six intelligences are "basic stock" on every human brain that comes off the assembly line. You draw on them every day to some degree (but in most cases, it's a very small degree).

As with swimming and driving a car, this program merely shows you how to use innate capabilities you already have. Those who make better use of all six intelligences learn to

- Write dynamic memos and reports that compel attention

- Express themselves confidently and tellingly in any situation

- Effortlessly sell others on their point of view

- Cut through paperwork and reading by absorbing memos, reports, and lengthy articles at a glance

- Become a "wizard of memory" who can mentally trap important data, facts, and figures and recall them long afterward

- See critical opportunities and answers other people routinely miss

- Find a solution to every professional, personal, and familial impasse—even those others consider unsolvable

- Tell infallibly when someone is trying to deceive, mislead, or manipulate them

- Keep ahead of competitors, minimizing setbacks and capitalizing on opportunities by foreseeing future events

- Tell which of their ideas are brilliant inspirations and which harebrained ideas

- Learn new jobs and physical tasks with astonishing facility

- Accomplish more with less, boosting output without boosting effort

- Understand what others are thinking and feeling without being told

- Navigate troubled professional or personal waters with emotional radar

THE POWER OF YOUR SIX INTELLIGENCES

It's important to emphasize that what we are talking about here is not different "components" of intelligence. They are six distinct, separate brain systems that evolved, and function, in separate convolutions of our gray matter. For instance, when a coach at a motivational seminar asks you a question, the verbal system understands the question, thinks about it, and arrives at a solution, all purely in the form of words, without stimulating the regions responsible for the visual, logical, the creative, the physical, or the emotional.

Conversely, when we trip in the dark while walking across our bedroom, the brain system governing the body grasps the situation, orients itself spatially, sorts through all the possible responses, and sends a hand out unerringly to a desk or headboard—all in a split second—and without the verbal, visual, creative, or emotional regions coming into play until afterward. In the same way, it's possible to solve a math problem utilizing only the logical faculty without bringing any of the other five systems into the equation at all.

Clearly, what we have going here, masquerading under the name "intelligence," is not the monolithic mental phenomenon we once thought. Nor are they merely different facets of the same phenomenon. For sometimes, such as when we are concentrating on something physical—playing football or cutting wooden scrollwork with a bandsaw—other regions of the mind are simultaneously preoccupied by different matters, like a failed relationship. When this happens, several intelligences are processing data and making judgments separately and at the same time.

In terms of raising your personal smarts, the implications of the preceding are enormous. Previous approaches to elevating intelligence have necessarily taken a piecemeal approach. They gave advice about either logical thinking or creativity. But, even those that concentrated on elevating other intelligences, such as emotional or visual smarts, still dealt with only a single intelligence. This left the vast portion of your potential mental capacities untapped. (The multiple-intelligences approach, however, focuses on raising all six.)

Following is a short sketch of each of the six intelligences, along with some of the miraculous benefits that go with unlocking them.

THE POWER OF YOUR VERBAL INTELLIGENCE

Your verbal intelligence, also known as "word smarts" and "linguistic intelligence," is the brain system responsible for everything to do with words. It enables you to remember them, understand them, think them, speak them, read them, and write them.

This is a major mental feat, and verbal intelligence takes up a significant volume of brain cells. And no wonder! It is a faculty we are called upon to use constantly throughout our day, playing a critical part in ensuring your professional and personal advancement. Every conversation, encounter, meeting, or conference draws on your word smarts whether you are the listener or the speaker.

Typically, we draw on less than 25 percent of our verbal intelligence. Even those who employ their word smarts constantly, such as writers and news commentators, rarely draw on more than 50 percent of their verbal IQ.

We all know people gifted in word smarts. It might be the award-winning saleswoman, who wins clients over with her inexhaustible fund of shaggy dog stories and spellbinding accounts of adventures as an army nurse. Or it might be the self-employed computer nerd, who makes $100,000 per year and always has his nose stuck in a magazine or book. Or it might be the CEO who soothes disputes using exceptional listening powers to find areas of commonality.

Because they think in words, those who are strong in word smarts were the teacher's pet in English and creative writing and learn most quickly through lectures and books. They are motivated to get started on any assignment that requires linguistic expertise or allows them to work with tools such as laptops, or poster paper for "clustering," that give their verbal intelligence a chance to play. They also tend to keep their verbal IQ maximized by reading, listening to audio books, journaling, word games, making puns, and writing poetry. People who have become famous by exercising their verbal intelligence include Maya Angelou, Tony Robbins, Robin Williams, Germaine Greer, Isaac Asimov, Mary Matalin, Geraldo Rivera, and Johnnie Cochran.

Power Professions Where Verbal IQ Counts

Word smarts play a central role in getting ahead in any field. No matter what your career path, you would be wise to expand on your verbal intelligence It is your ticket to the top in careers such as the following, which depend on the ability to effectively employ words.

- Journalist, novelist, poet, playwright, editor
- Advertising sparkplug, sales rep, marketing director, spin doctor
- Stand-up comedian, humorist, news commentator
- Restaurateur, hotelier, publican
- Politician, clergyperson, motivational speaker
- Attorney, judge, paralegal
- Translator, diplomat, mediator
- Teacher, educator, mentor
- Psychotherapist, counselor, facilitator
- Television anchor, disc jockey, talk-show host
- Publisher, printer, bookstore owner

Even if you are not someone whose strong suit lies in his or her verbal IQ, you can achieve the kind of verbal mastery shared by those in the preceding professions by putting some effort into expanding your word smarts. Days 1 to 4 of this program will provide you with techniques designed to help you do precisely that.

THE POWER OF YOUR VISUAL INTELLIGENCE

Visual intelligence, also known as "picture smarts," is the brain system responsible for processing and storing all visual images, real and "imaginary." Sight is such an all-encompassing aspect of our daily lives that the portion of brain matter allocated to visual intelligence outweighs that of verbal intelligence.

After all, we make use of our vision from the moment when we wake until we retire at night. It's in operation when we turn on the shower, put on makeup or shave, eat our breakfast, make the commute to the office, and throughout the workday—navigating the halls, operating the copier, filling out a form, or simply daydreaming—right on to playing squash, watching television, and searching the web in the evening. The brain systems responsible for verbal intelligence are on overdrive so much of the day that they are still processing information while we sleep, manifesting themselves in the form of vivid, motion-picture-like dreams.

Yet, paradoxically, beyond the act of seeing some of what is around us, this is one of the most underused intelligences. For, we look but we do not see. Can you describe what the person you rode next to on the subway this morning was wearing? If you were an artist, or someone else who developed his or picture smarts, you could.

Because they think in images and can picture things vividly in their minds, those with picture smarts received straight As in art and geometry and respond best to information and lessons presented in visual form. They perform at their peak when jobs cry out for visual IQ, such as charts, slides, video. They keep their visual intelligence high with eye-teasing pastimes such as jigsaw puzzles, doodling, mazes, movies, gardening, art exhibits, photography, and coffee-table books. Among those whose picture smarts led to notable accomplishments are: Stephen Spielberg, Jane Goodall, Annie Lebowitz, Claes Oldenburg, Spike Lee, Andy Warhol, and Dr. Seuss.

Power Professions Where Visual IQ Counts

All professions are dependent on our capacity for sight. Well-developed picture smarts are your key to advancement in any career. So visual intelligence is important, no matter what your job. But certain occupations draw more heavily on visual IQ than do others, and those who work there have a higher degree than do most of us. These careers include

- Mechanic, inventor, engineer, electrician
- Sailor, pilot, astronaut, race-car driver
- Athlete, acrobat, jockey, daredevil
- Surgeon, paramedic, radiologist
- Paleontologist, anthropologist, geologist
- Photographer, sculptor, painter
- Architect, cartographer, genealogist
- Television, motion-picture or theatrical director or producer; photographer; actor; lighting or scenic designer
- Cinematographer, photographer of video and film
- Fashion designer, hairdresser, makeup artist
- Guide, scout, soldier

After you have completed the portion of this program (days 5 through 7) focused on raising your visual IQ, you can raise your picture smarts to the genius level, too.

THE POWER OF YOUR LOGICAL INTELLIGENCE

Logical intelligence is also known as "thinking smarts," "the problem-solving intelligence," "conscious decision making." Our power to reason and think logically is not only what separates us from the beasts. It is also responsible for all human progress and has brought us from the stone age through the iron and steel ages to the digital age.

Every second in life requires a decision or poses a problem. It begins with which side of the bed to get out of, encompasses how to pay for your son's new braces, which of yesterday's unanswered letters to begin with when you settle in at your desk for the morning, the best way to get that promotion, whether to invest in a nationally known franchise or start a new restaurant on your own, even what to make for dinner at night. About the only time your thinking smarts aren't on the line, having to make choices and reach decisions every minute, is while you sleep.

So it makes sense that the volume of human brain matter given over to logical intelligence far exceeds that of any other animal's. If the brain weren't able to assign extraordinary resources to logical intelligence, we would never be able to keep up with the constant barrage of choices, large and small, we are required to make each waking minute. Nor would so many of them work out in our favor. (It may not always seem that way, because it's natural to focus on the mistakes you make and overlook the much vaster number of choices that turn out right. After all, you probably have a job, a home, disposable income, and leisure time, or you wouldn't be reading this book. So you can't be any mental pigmy, and you have plenty of thinking smarts to spare.)

Because they think in logical connections and numbers, individuals who possess thinking smarts earned top grades in science and math and learn best when they can assemble the information they need in a logical fashion. They become fired with passion for assignments that challenge their problem-solving or organizational know-how. They keep their logical IQ optimized by attending professional workshops on weekends and taking courses toward an advanced degree during vacations. Thinking smarts put these people at the pinnacles of their professions: Barbara Walters, Carl Sagan, Marilyn vos Savant, John H. Johnson, Bill Gates, Alan Keyes, and Rosabeth Moss Kantor.

Power Professions Where Logical IQ Counts

Anything with a business aspect—and that's almost every profession—clearly demands thinking smarts. Unlocking your logical intelligence is the key to success in virtually all areas of life. It is even more crucial when your interests take you toward becoming a

- Scientist: biologist, physicist, chemist, astronomer, zoologist
- Physician, medical researcher, laboratory technician
- Computer designer, programmer, repair technician
- Mathematician, statistician, accountant, CPA
- Banker, financial analyst, market-fund manager, stock broker

- Clerk, cashier, bank teller
- Time-management, performance, productivity or systems analyst
- Personal assistant, secretary, office manager

You can expand your thinking smarts to the same degree as those in the preceding professions. The exercises presented on days 8 to 11 of this program will show you ways you can resource all your logical intelligence.

THE POWER OF YOUR CREATIVE INTELLIGENCE

Creative intelligence, also known as "idea smarts," "originality," and "inventive intelligence," is behind every new idea and daydream you get, from how to stop that sudden leak under the sink long enough to get through a dinner party, how to tactfully tell a colleague about his bad breath, what to do with those three million semiconductors purchasing accidentally ordered, how to be on time for that meeting during a citywide taxi strike, or the best way to say "I'm sorry" to a loved one. Creativity is such a natural human trait and a vital part of our existence that we take it for granted and rarely notice it's in operation most of the time we are making use of our idea smarts. Our ancestors needed an ample share when they were wandering from cave to cave on the savannas, with every moment bringing a new danger or a new opportunity. And the brain's creativity intelligence grew until we were an ingenious species, never failing to come up with an ingenious solution to our difficulties.

Creative intelligence lies behind every new innovation and advance. Logic may have worked out the method of striking flint against iron-bearing rock to spark a fire, but it was creativity that envisioned having a fire blazing in the midst of the encampment in the first place. It also lies behind every innovation in business, from the Windows operating system to the multinational corporation.

Because they experience a constant flow of original thoughts and inspirations, those with idea smarts flourish in classes such as theater, design, and television; catch fire for jobs that demand inventiveness; and maintain their edge by attending movies and concerts, or through writing, directing, or painting themselves. People whose creative IQs made them household names include Thomas Edison, Martha Stewart, Barbra Streisand, Warren Bennis, Oprah Winfrey, Warren Buffett, and Stephen Hawking.

Power Professions Where Creative IQ Counts

People usually think of acting, writing, or advertising when they think of careers that require ample idea smarts. But every job calls for a dash of your creative IQ now and then: the nurse who needs a way to coax a bandage on a cranky child, the manager who is asked to meet tougher quotas while cutting personnel, the shopkeeper whose window display must catch the customer's eye. Creative intelligence is especially important, however, when your career goals include any of the following:

- Entrepreneur, small-business owner, CEO
- Graphic arts: illustrator, photographer, designer
- Inventor, creator, idea person
- Manager and marketer of art and artists
- Electronic media: radio, television, cable, video
- Live theater: plays, performance art, improv comedy
- Music: singer, instrumentalist, composer
- Landscaper, architect, community planner
- Advertising, marketing, salesperson
- Fashion designer, cosmetician, coiffeur
- Toy and game designer, children's books and records artist

It takes surprisingly little time or effort to get started increasing your idea smarts and acquiring the creative finesse that can make you a winner in these careers, or in any others. You will begin building yours in only three days (days 12 through 14 of the program).

THE POWER OF YOUR PHYSICAL INTELLIGENCE

Physical intelligence, also known as "body smarts," is the brain complex that oversees every bodily activity, internal and external. Since you have already gone through the entire process involved in purchasing this book, getting it home, sitting down to read, and have reached this page, you ought to have some notion of why the body needs its own separate brain system and intelligence. If your rational, conscious self tried to keep track of all the stuff going on at home and the office, while supervising every step and move you make, it would have a breakdown.

Yet, for all its obvious importance, and for all the obvious brain power delegated to it, most of us never make any real attempt to elevate our physical IQ. Despite the evidence before our eyes, we fall prey to the misperception that all body smarts aren't useful unless someone becomes an athlete and performer. That this attitude might be saddling us with an enormous handicap never crosses our mind.

Because they think with their bodies, people with body smarts are noticeably well-coordinated and graceful, excel in physical education, and were probably on one team or another (or had musical talent and played in the school band). They typically throw themselves wholeheartedly into any effort that can engage their physical intelligence, and they maintain their physical IQ with activities such as racquetball and backpacking. Any list of individuals who owe their achievements to expanded body smarts would have to include Eddie Murphy, Dean Edell, Colin Powell, Martina Navratilova, "Dr. Ruth" Westheimer, Babe Ruth, and Fred Astaire.

Power Professions Where Physical IQ Counts

Being fit and the ability to learn new skills are as important to the office worker as to the dock worker. Most careers demand stamina, dexterity, coordination, and that you be in tune with your own body. But those involved in any of the following careers find their physical IQ in constant demand:

- Singer, actor, "slapstick" comedian
- Craftsperson, jeweler, computer repairperson
- Plumber, mechanic, carpenter
- Butcher, gardener, anyone who works with his or her hands
- Chauffeur, truck driver, airline pilot
- Gymnast, ballplayer, swimmer, ice skater
- Dancer, ballerina, martial artist
- Sculptor, muralist
- Law enforcement officer, anyone serving in the military, firefighter
- Surgeon, nurse, paramedic
- Naturalist, veterinarian, animal trainer
- Archeologist, anthropologist, archeologist

If the type of body smarts these people possess sounds as if they would enhance your life, it's only two short weeks away. Days 15 to 17 will lead through exercises designed to jump-start your physical intelligence.

THE POWER OF YOUR EMOTIONAL INTELLIGENCE

Emotional intelligence, also known as "feeling smarts," encompasses the entire emotional realm. Personal life is about nothing if not emotion, from our own enjoyment of a winter landscape, the love of others for us, or the anger of strained communications. But they are an often overlooked factor in business. Motivation, after all, is an emotional charge that gets us up out of our chair eager to get something done, and a superior's anger can be a frightening thing when you have bills to pay, while a feeling that "we all respect each other and can get along" is essential to the continued productivity of any organization.

Emotions tell us to be frightened and run away when threatened by danger and light us up with warmth to draw us toward the protections of fellowship with others. We typically never consider just how extensive the emotional realm is or just how many of the brain's two hundred billion cells must be given over to the circuits responsible just for handling our feelings. Getting the most out of those circuits would be like turning up the light by several billion watts.

Because they do their best thinking and problem solving in terms of feelings, those with feeling smarts were popular in school and belonged to the student council, debating team, or dramatic society; are best motivated by assignments that require them to interact heavily with others; learn quickest from coaches and mentors; and educate their emotional IQ with group games, social gatherings, community events, and mentoring.

Included in the many world-class figures who made it on their emotional intelligence are Jesse Jackson, Dr. Joy Browne, Steven Covey, Mary Kay Ash, Barney Frank, Lisa Ling, Les Brown, and Conrad Hilton.

Power Professions Where Emotional IQ Counts

Feeling smarts is a real plus in any job. Getting along with colleagues and managers always calls for a deft interpersonal touch and a positive attitude toward others. It's wise to keep your emotional intelligence at its peak if you are in positions that involve extensive personal interactions with the public, such as

- Teacher, mentor, consultant
- Politician, attorney, minister
- Psychologist, peer counselor, social worker
- Marketing person, salesperson, public relations person
- Customer service manager, receptionist, greeter
- Negotiator, mediator, conflict manager
- Manager, administrator, team leader

You will find exercises for germinating many abilities possessed by the preceding on days 18 to 21, which conclude this three-week program.

FIVE MINI-EXERCISES THAT PROVE THE VALUE OF THIS PROGRAM

Usually, by the time I reach this point in telling audiences about the six intelligences and how boosting them can give people super brain power, the vast majority of the participants begin to stare at me as if I were crazy. They are willing to believe that other people can somehow master these skills, but they aren't willing to believe that they themselves can learn them, too.

Yet, just a few minutes and a few simple exercises later, even those with the strongest doubts are thrilled to discover that they have, indeed, tapped undreamed of potentials. They find that's all it takes to begin drawing on their hidden genius. By the time the weekend is over, participants are accessing 50 percent and more of each of their six intelligences. They no longer doubt that "super brain power" is more than a slogan and are well along on the path to achieving it.

But you don't need to take anyone else's word for this. You can put it the test right now. Following are six simple, but powerful mini-exercises. None appear elsewhere in the book. (Look upon them as a bonus, just for reading this far in the chapter.)

Each of these techniques will grant you increased access to one of your six intelligences. I challenge you to select one of these exercises and put it to use right now, in your own life. I believe that like my workshop participants, you will be impressed by the difference it makes. So impressed, in fact, that you'll have the motivation to start this program and stay with it the entire three weeks, until you have fully unlocked your hidden genius.

1. *Super-sizing your verbal intelligence.* This technique is very powerful, for all of its seeming straightforwardness. You don't even have to go out of your way or do anything special to make it work. Yet, this exercise will help you become sensitive to verbal clues other people give that unconsciously reveal what's important to them. It will also start you on the way toward becoming sensitive to how, by selecting certain kinds of words, you can enormously heighten the effect of what you say has on others.

Over the next twenty-four hours, as you listen to people, focus on the words they use when they are being emotional. These words will be more vivid and have stronger impact. They also contain key verbal elements that you can use to express emotion when you want to impress on people that what you are saying is important to you.

Much of the time what people are saying will be just surrounding detail and consist of flat recitation of facts—little more than nouns and verbs. "It wasn't anything different at the meeting. Just cut-and-dry figures." *The parts that matter to the other person typically contain descriptive, "emotional" adjectives and adverbs.*

Examples: "But I discovered that we can give your company a *terrific* deal on our *top-of-the line* copy machine. It's been a *runaway bestseller,* and we've *significantly* reduced unit costs by outsourcing to Taiwan. That means a *super* cut in price to you, the *lucky* wholesaler." Or, "All of a *sudden* I realized something *electrifying.* Our department is this year's *fair-haired* gal! We are generating an *astonishing* percentage of this year's profits. That makes it a *slam-dunk* to get *hefty* raises for us all." Or even, "Jake, you won't believe how *awful* this is. It's a *total calamity.* The *d——ed* car engine blew up."

Once you become accustomed to listening for these kinds of "verbal clues," you will find yourself spotting almost automatically what is meaningful to the other person. This is particularly useful in negotiations, sales efforts, and any time you need to find what motivates or excites someone else. It will also lead you to an increased awareness of the kind of emotionally powerful words you can use to motivate others.

2. *Super-sizing your visual intelligence.* This exercise will expand on your natural capacity to store and retrieve images from your visual data banks (that is, remember whatever you see). It takes only a short time, and you do it anywhere, at the office or at home.

Select a drawer you know contains a miscellany of items—a desk drawer or a hardware drawer—but don't open it, yet. First, get a timer and set it for fifteen seconds. Next, take a deep breath, let it out, and relax. Start the timer, then open the drawer and look at what's in it until the fifteen seconds are up. Close the drawer. Now take out a sheet of paper and write down everything you can remember seeing inside it. Then, open the drawer again and in a separate column list everything there that you forgot you saw or that you got wrong. (In a variant, you can just close your eyes after walking into a new room, for instance, and attempt to visualize everything you have just seen.)

Ultimately, this will strengthen your knack for recalling visual details of every stripe, from who attended meetings, to graphs, memos, and reports.

3. *Super-sizing your creative intelligence.* Want in on the best-kept secret about creative inspirations? Most of the world's most celebrated strokes of genius came to people while they were relaxed in a chair, stretched out comfortably on a sofa, or in some other condition of repose. Pick a dilemma that really has you stuck, whether it's super brain power related or a personal concern, one where you could really do with a creative inspiration. Lean back, close your eyes, take a deep breath, let your mind go blank. Now breathe in and out easily and without strain. After a while, ideas and images centered around your subject will begin to percolate through your brain. Don't attempt to write them down or make sense of them. Just let your thoughts wander comfortably around the topic. After a while you will notice that your thoughts are starting to take on a pattern or to center on a single theme. Again, don't attempt to write them down. You are in no hurry. But eventually most people find their thoughts beginning to knit themselves together into exactly the answer they were seeking.

4. *Super-sizing your physical intelligence.* Pick something with a physical component that you have had difficulty learning before—whether it's which data go in what fields on your new marketing software or the proper way to flick a flyreel.

First, tighten the muscles of your body until they are all very hard, especially the ones you will be using most. Maintaining this state, take about five minutes and actually try to perform the task. Then stop. You will probably notice that your movements were awkward, and uncoordinated, that you did no better, if not worse, than the last time you tried. You may also notice that you felt tired afterward and that your muscles ached afterward.

You were probably already anxious about or even dreading this particular learning experience the first time you approached it, and you probably tightened up physically like this, too. For some reason, most people labor under the misapprehension that when performing a physical activity they should tense all their muscles to exert maximum physical effort. But when you tighten the muscles like this, they begin to get in each other's way. Knotted muscles not only perform with less grace and coordination, their stiffness resists the smooth, efficient interplay of the other muscles. Naturally, you can't perform your best under such circumstances. (Tensing the muscles also releases various stress hormones, including cortisol, which interfere with learning by impairing both the short- and the long-term memory systems critical to learning.)

Start all over. But this time, take a deep breath and relax completely. Instead of concentrating hard on learning and on tightening up your body for maximum effort, just start "playing around" with the task. If you're learning to use a new keyboard, for instance, don't try for accuracy—try for fun. Try to have fun with the keys: Start by typing out a rhythm like a piano, or maybe strike them in with your fingers in a funny way, like Chico Marx at the piano. Or make up a silly song with a simple rhythm, and wag your head or body to it with each separate key you strike. Something like, "The unit cost is in the upper left-hand green field—Oh! And the customer price is in the lower center green one—Oh!" (hitting the key with each "oh").

When you have played with the task like this for a while, stop. Review how you've done, and take stock of how you feel. Probably, your fingering of the keyboard was less stiff and clumsy, and you probably feel significantly more relaxed and energized than you did the first time around. And oddly, for all that you were goofing around with the task, you probably made less mistakes this time, too.

Now, staying relaxed, return to the task again. You will probably be dumbfounded to discover that you are doing much better. Remember, being relaxed and making a game of it heightens your likelihood of remembering what you are learning and liberates your muscles to perform at their best.

5. *Super-sizing your emotional intelligence.* Here is a remarkably effort-free method for getting in touch with your emotions in any situation. It will alert you to unconscious feelings you can use as a guide to making decisions of every stripe.

Typically, emotions can manifest and make themselves known anywhere in the body—a soaring heart, knotted stomach, weak knees, cold hands, prickling scalp. But for most people, feelings first begin to manifest in one particular spot. The location of this "signal" spot varies from person to person, and you may already know where yours is located. However, if you are not aware of where your emotional "signal" spot is, this technique will help you find it.

Sit down, close your eyes and relax. Mentally review how your body feels. Try to tune in onto any region that feels tense, a set of muscles that are knotted, a region that seems "tingly," or one that seems cold or even warm. This is your emotional "signal" spot. Your emotional responses to situations, and to your life over all, will manifest there first.

Over the next few days, as you interact with others at the workplace and in your personal life or when you find yourself in a challenging or difficult situation, keep checking in on this signal spot. When it feels "good" or "warm," your emotional intelligence is sending you a positive signal about the situation; when it feels tense, knotted, or "cold," your feelings are warning you that your deep psyche has identified a negative element your conscious mind has missed.

If you have put just one of these mini-exercises into practice, you are probably amazed at the results—at just how much your mental acuity has been enhanced. And, you are probably eager to turn the page to Day 1 and begin work right away on expanding your own verbal intelligence.

The First Key—

UNLOCKING YOUR VERBAL GENIUS

WHAT'S YOUR VERBAL IQ?

The following self-assessment quiz will help you determine your verbal intelligence quotient. If it is currently weaker than you would like, don't despair. On each of the first four days of this program, you will learn simple, but powerful techniques designed to help build your verbal muscles. Even if you are naturally possessed of an ample share of word smarts, I still recommend you perform each day's exercise as a refresher, which will not only hone your skills with words, but will also make you aware of how to use them or benefit from them in a new way.

To find your verbal IQ, check any phrases that apply. Do you

☐ Think in words, rather than in pictures or sensations?

☑ Like to play with words while talking or writing: tongue twisters, nonsense rhymes, double entendres, alliteration, puns?

☑ Get better grades in English and history than in math and science?

☐ Keep a diary or some kind of journal?

☑ Enjoy good conversation and arguing your points?

☑ Have a fondness for telling anecdotes, spinning shaggy-dog stories, making jokes?

☑ Carry a notebook or pocket tape recorder at all times to jot down important ideas?

☑ Listen to audio books while driving?

☐ Have your head frequently stuck in a magazine, newspaper, or book?

☐ Enjoy giving presentations at company meetings, trade shows, seminars?

☐ Compulsively read cereal boxes, soup-can labels, or old magazines in waiting rooms?

☑ Like to write reports, articles, brochures, memos?

☑ Have curiosity about things like the meanings or origins of words, phrases, names, or popular expressions?

☐ "Hear" the words you are going to say in your head before you say them?

☑ Delight in clever use of the sounds, rhythms, inflections, and meters of words, the way some people delight in sunsets and mountain vistas?

☑ Enjoy attending workshops, seminars, or lectures with a particularly fascinating speaker?

☐ Pass time playing word games such as Scrabble, Hangman, Anagrams, or Password?

☑ Find you are more apt at English grammar than most people you know?

☐ Have a yearning to write poetry, plays, short stories, a novel, or a fact-based book?

☑ Spend time using word-processing programs and looking things up on the internet?

Scoring: Add up the number of boxes you checked. If your score was between 1 and 4, your verbal muscles haven't had much exercise. But, don't worry! Today's exercise (on the following page) will immediately begin to develop your verbal intelligence. By the time you have completed the fourth day's exercise, your word smarts will be well on the up-curve.

If your score was between 5 and 11, you aren't getting even half the benefit of your full verbal IQ. But, as of today, that is going to change. Four days from now, after completing the following four exercises, you will discover you have a vastly expanded verbal intelligence.

If your score was between 12 and 16, you have a higher verbal IQ than most people, enjoy talking, writing, reading, word games, but there is still room for improvement. Develop your word smarts to the max with the exercises that follow.

If your score was between 17 and 20, you are at the top of the class! You are probably already earning your living in some career where being so strong in word smarts gives you critical leverage. In that case, you won't need any encouragement to try the exercises that follow. You will want to do them just for the fun of it.

UNLOCKING YOUR VERBAL INTELLIGENCE

Welcome to the initial four days of the program, which focus on the first of the six keys: verbal intelligence. The super brain power program begins with verbal intelligence, because it is being presented in the form of a book. This way, if you are someone low in word smarts, who doesn't absorb information so readily through reading, you will be able to go into the rest of the book with the problem already remedied. Then you'll be in a better position to get the most out of what you read. (You'll find today's exercise immediately following these brief introductory pages.)

If you have completed the self-quiz on page 29, you already know your verbal IQ. If it's not all you wish it to be at the present moment, it soon will be. When you finish these first four days, you will be well on your way to fully developing your verbal muscles. If you are someone who tested near the top in verbal intelligence, you are the kind of person who loves playing with words so much you're probably already champing at the bit to give them a try.

HOW AN M.D. SALVAGED A CAREER BY DEVELOPING HER VERBAL IQ

Razyia had been born and received her M.D. in India. Then she met and married a vacationing astronomer from the University of Massachusetts and moved to the United States. Although Razyia had graduated at the top of her class in Calcutta, she kept flunking the exam required to practice medicine in her newly adopted country.

We met at one of my seminars, and Razyia asked me if I thought the standards of American medicine were so much higher than those in India that, while she had shone in her home country, she couldn't pass even a basic licensing exam over here.

My reply surprised her. I asked if she had ever taken an intelligence test while attending school in Calcutta and, if so, how high her score had been.

Razyia told me she had been given an Indian IQ test and that she had scored in the 170 range.

I asked her if she had a computer. Razyia said she did, and I suggested she log on to one of several websites where you could take the standard U.S. IQ test and then phone her score to me.

Razyia sounded crushed when she called me back with the score. She had barely managed a 135. "Was I just coasting by because our tests in India are so much easier?" she asked.

I quickly reassured her that I believed that the tests in India were probably just as rigorous as those in the United States. The fact that Razyia had shown so poorly in both the medical and the IQ tests suggested a common link.

I suggested Razyia wait a year before going back for her licensing exam. In the meantime, I urged her to enroll in a writing course and try a conscious technique for expanding her English vocabulary. Today, having successfully passed the exam, Razyia is happily engaged in the practice of medicine in the state of California. (And by the way, Razyia retook an IQ test, too, and this time scored in the 170 range.)

What was the connection between Razyia's failure to pass the medical licensing exam and her low score on the intelligence test?

The answer is: Her command of the English language. You see, what IQ tests primarily measure is verbal intelligence. More specifically, they gauge the person's verbal IQ in the language the test is printed in.

HOW RAISING YOUR WORD SMARTS CAN RAISE YOUR "OFFICIAL" IQ

While most people believe that regular IQ tests (typically, the Stanford-Binet in the United States) measure logical intelligence because "being smart" seems to involve thinking logically and problem solving, this is a misconception. What most intelligence tests measure best isn't logical—or even general—intelligence, but verbal intelligence. After all, most of the questions and answers on the tests are in the form of words, aren't they?

Looked at another way, then, what intelligence tests actually determine is how well you have developed your word smarts. If you haven't exercised them much, you won't score very high. But, if you are someone who has been exercising them all your life, you are likely to place in the upper percentiles.

This means raising your verbal IQ can actually raise your Stanford-Binet score.

WHY EXPERTS SAY RAISING YOUR VERBAL IQ IS KEY TO SUCCESS

How important is increasing your word smarts? Success gurus, from Tony Robbins to Marianne Williamson, all acknowledge the importance of a strong, well-exercised verbal intelligence. As Dr. Wilfred Funk, educator and founder of the Funk and Wagnalls publishing firm, writes, "After a host of experiments and years of testing . . . practical, hardheaded scientists, have found out . . . that one of the quickest and easiest ways to get ahead . . . is by consciously building up your knowledge of words."

Management consultant James K. Van Fleet, author of *Dynamics of Motivation*, concurs and even identifies word smarts as *the* central component in success. "All other things being equal, advancement and promotion will invariably go to the person who has mastered the art of self-expression, both in speaking and writing, while his colleague who attaches little or no importance to what can be achieved with the use of language, will be marked for mediocrity or failure."

EIGHT POWERS YOU GAIN WHEN YOU SUPER-SIZE YOUR WORD SMARTS

People who are long on word smarts possess a number of valuable abilities that are key to success in some areas of life. They have a "gift of gab" or an incisive flair for expressing themselves through the written word—most often both. Frequently, they are avid readers, devouring the newest Stephen King or Rita Mae Brown opus or *Newsweek* at a single sitting. They all have a facility for using words to get their point across successfully to others, usually buttressing it with a wealth of supporting knowledge they've picked up over the years.

They are often found among self-made millionaires, executives, academics, professionals, computer programmers, and the arts. Half in envy, we call them "bookworms" or dub them someone "in love with the sound of their own words." Psychiatrists classify them as "verbally oriented." Academics classify them as having "linguistic intelligence" or "verbal intelligence."

If we envy people who are strong in word smarts, it is not hard to understand. They have so many wonderful verbal gifts that are underpinnings to success. Achievement consultants like Warren Bennis and Mary Kay Ash have identified eight ways that a high verbal IQ can empower people.

When you have unlocked the power of your own verbal intelligence, you too will be able to:

1. *Write documents that compel attention.* Unleash the power of words to express yourself lucidly, concisely, dramatically. Have a world-class vocabulary without trying. Use "power phrases" and "telling" words to make your ideas stand out. Pen blockbuster memos, reports, summaries, speeches, articles, advertising circulars, brochures, newsletters, even books, that make things happen and score big kudos with your bosses and colleagues. Create an attention-grabbing resume that gets you the job as quality-control technician at the cereal factory. Get your point across and stir others to take action with every word you write. Pen the memo that convinces your bosses to fix the bottleneck in production that's been a thorn in the side of the marketing department for years. Tell the story of the Kosovo refugees so movingly in the church newsletter that people dig down and make serious contributions, even though April 15 is only a few weeks away. Pen the speech that gets you elected president of your local Chamber of Commerce.

2. *Sell anyone on your proposals, products, and ideas.* Use the power of words to make your case and persuade others. Gain agreement from even the stubbornest people. Transform "no's" into "yes's" almost at once. Overcome doubts and objections, convincing others of your position. Win over the chain-store buyer who has always refused to do business with your company. Persuade your boss to give you that raise. Convince the hostile clerk to take back the new shirt you never took out of the box. Persuade your stubborn neighbor to vote your way on the co-op board.

3. *Shine in conversation and give dynamite speeches.* Use the power of words to add luster to oral presentations. Say what you mean to say, in the way you want to say it. Make the dull interesting and the muddled clear. Know what to say so people listen to you and give your words greater weight than they do others. Elicit instant respect and cooperation from disgruntled salesclerks, stubborn bureaucrats, indifferent waiters, unhappy relatives. Make points intelligently and interestingly around the watercooler and the dinner table. Leave a favorable impression from the way you present a summary for a conference, offer off-the-cuff insights at a meeting, or pull off a formal speech. Make clear to a consistently tardy worker that you won't tolerate any further lateness. Deliver the presentation that awakens your partners to the serious defect in their current website. Craft the campaign that puts your new restaurant on the map. Untangle the misunderstanding between your sister and your aunt.

4. *Zip through documents and retain the important details.* Use the power of words to assimilate information from books, articles, memos, reports, newspapers, magazines, and webpages with ease. Read complicated manuals and reports in one fourth the time, with twice the understanding. Recall anything you've read for years. Finally get around to reading that management book your boss touted so highly. Zip through that report on cotton production in Turkey you thought would take all weekend, on Friday night—and still have Saturday and Sunday to play. Pass that English Lit exam. Back up your argument with that colleague on the internet about the magnesium industry by citing the telling fact you read two years earlier.

5. *Win friends and allies in social situations.* Use the power of words to make the most of social interactions and opportunities. Gain the esteem and support of others by what you say and when you say it. Strike up new friendships at parties, seminars, conventions, athletic events, concerts, the theater. Say just the right thing to earn the approval of your prospective in-laws. Be a hit at your new client's party. Get a long-hoped-for recommendation to an elusive prospect from someone you just met at the semiconductor conference. Intrigue that interesting someone you have just spotted across the room.

6. *See through attempts at verbal deception.* Use the power of words to reveal attempts by others to manipulate language and distort or conceal information. Notice quickly just where the gimmick lies in commercials, telemarketing promotions, magazine solicitations, home-repair offers, and other scams. Spot hidden agendas in articles and speeches. Become a verbal lie-detector who can always tell truth from lie. On second reading of the contract, decide not to sign and sink $175,000 in savings into the muffler franchise. Know if the new vice president of international relations is sincere when she announces that you in particular will not be a victim of downsizing. Catch the mistake your son makes that reveals the real truth about how the bicycle got broken.

7. *Listen with "antennae" ears and remember everything you hear.* Use the power of words to strengthen hearing and evoke memories and association. Hear "between the lines." Understand what people are "really" saying. Focus in on and retain all the essentials when information is presented at conferences, meetings, even casual conversation. Remember the name of that potential contact you met at the publishing convention, whose business card you've lost. Report back to your colleagues virtually every memorable phrase from the Zig Ziglar seminar you just attended. Be the one whose name comes up first as a replacement when your manager retires, because you always have the right information at your fingertips. Hear the subtle clues revealing that that special someone feels the same way about you.

8. *Solve most problems easily with laser-sharp thinking.* Use the power of words to formulate thoughts with precision. Distinguish yourself in any organization or group for your talent for solving problems that stump others. Easily keep abreast of competitors, changing trends, challenges. Spot shoddy thinking, fallacies, and lapses in logic. Overcome whatever obstacles life throws your way. Discover a technique for simplifying the school district's purchasing policy that saves thousands of dollars per year. Find the way to make your classical station thrive in a market where only rock and country are succeeding. Think of a strategy that allows you and your spouse to afford that summer home in Vermont.

HOW YOU CAN BOOST YOUR WORD SMARTS

If you are someone who has always envisioned him or herself as deficient in word smarts, then you probably have difficulty expressing yourself, get a headache trying to follow involved speeches, find it slow going when you have to plow through pages and pages of words. You may have difficulty believing you can ever become a dynamic speaker or an excellent writer.

But don't forget, verbal intelligence isn't something that some of us have and others were shorted in. It's something you were born with, hardwired throughout a large section of brain.

You already have a larger share of word smarts than you probably give yourself credit for or are even aware you have. You've already learned to speak and write what linguists worldwide admit is one of the most difficult languages to master (English!). You know hundreds of words and can make yourself understood by most people in most situations. You have some storytelling ability, and have doubtless made jokes people laughed at. You have even probably learned to understand those complicated instructions translated literally from another language—the ones that explain how to work your VCR.

Like any other muscle group, if your verbal intelligence doesn't receive much of a workout, it will be weak and flabby and won't have much power. You probably doubt you could ever lift a hundred pounds or get through all the reading needed to get your MBA. But, put your body and mind through a regular series of workouts and at the end of a year you can lift a hundred pounds, or speed-read, with ease.

But is word power really that much like muscle power? Can someone actually build word smarts? Isn't that getting just a bit far-fetched? Before you decide, consider these two well-known examples, from among millions who have consciously set out to develop their verbal muscle group and succeeded in doing exactly that: Joseph Corned, for whom English was a second language, but who taught himself his adopted tongue so well that he became a best-selling novelist famed for his style; or Dale Carnegie, the shy young man with the stutter, who came "straight from a Missouri farm," and who trained himself to be one of the world's most celebrated public speakers.

You may not consider yourself much of a conversationalist now. And you may be ready to swear that you could never be a writer or much of a reader. But Sylvester Stallone was a sickly boy when he began working out, and by sticking with a program of rigorous exercises he built himself into a giant of strength. Stick with a program for building word smarts and you can be a giant in verbal intelligence, too.

FIVE PROVEN STRATEGIES FOR UNLOCKING YOUR VERBAL IQ

After you experience the positive results produced by the word smarts portion of this program, you will probably be curious about other ways of sharpening your verbal intelligence. Here are five proven ideas:

1. If you are one of those people who always seem to lose a verbal dispute and only later think of what you could have said to defend and put over your own point of view, take heart. Here is a painless technique for developing the ability to be a fluent and persuasive debater. When this happens, write down what you feel you should have said. Do this every time for a few weeks or months. It will help jump-start your mind's innate capacity for thinking on your feet verbally. By then you should find the replies you should be making to others popping into your mind during the discussion, and not afterward. You will also find that writing down your opinions helps boost your confidence for saying them out loud in front of others.

2. There are numerous magazines devoted to word games: acrostics, scrambled sentences, and crosswords. Purchase a few and give them a try. They will do more than anything else to raise your verbal intelligence.

3. Exercise your verbal dexterity the way musicians develop digital dexterity—by exercising frequently. Cajole friends into playing word games with you, or get a computer version of Scrabble or Hangman.

4. Pick a book that has also been issued as an audiocassette and as a movie, television show or video. First, watch the movie or television version, then listen to it on audiocassette, and finally read the book itself. This will stretch your verbal muscles and help you make connection between the different forms words can take. In addition, as Norman Lewis, author of *30 Days to a More Powerful Vocabulary* says, "Going from one form of language to another can develop and enrich verbal intelligence."

5. If you are a bit of a bibliophobe, someone who "doesn't like books" and finds reading itself a bit of a bore and a bit of a chore, psychologist Aidan Chamber may have a way to turn you completely around. Pick an article from a newspaper or magazine that touches on a personal passion of yours. On a sheet of paper make five columns; label them (1) "subject," (2) "liked," (3) "disliked," (4) "questions," (5) "learned." Read the article. As you encounter each new subject, jot it down in the first column in a word or two. Then jot down in the other column whether you liked or disliked what your read and any questions about the subject that left you wondering and/or anything worthwhile your learned. You will find *any* response you have to what you read deepens your emotional involvement with the process and turns it into an intimate, pleasurable experience, creating an appetite for reading.

PUTTING THE POWER OF WORDS TO WORK FOR YOU

The first day's exercise, presented on the following page, will help you begin unlocking your hidden genius by showing you how to turn even the simplest writing skills into a talent for coining power phrases for attention-grabbing memos, letters, and resumes. The second day's exercise will develop the ability you already have to make yourself understood in English and to transform it into a knack for speaking in a relaxed, interesting manner that holds listeners' attention and gets your ideas across. The third day's exercise will heighten your capacity for hearing and understanding words, until you instinctively pinpoint and remember all essential information at conferences, lectures, and meetings. The fourth day's exercise will show you how to supersize your ability to read so that you begin to whiz through newspapers, magazines, books, reports, memos, and other printed material, up to three times faster, immediately.

DAY 1 ————————————————————————————————
EXERCISE: POWER PHRASES

Right now, today, this minute, you are going to begin developing super brain power by exercising your inborn ability to put words together dramatically and tellingly. You may not believe you have this ability. But, after you have finished today's exercise, you will already have acquired the verbal flexibility and intelligence to express yourself with "power phrases." These are short combinations of words put together for maximum effect, so that they snare other people's attention by encapsulating your ideas in clear, vivid form.

The power phrases exercise is so simple, you don't even have to expand your vocabulary and memorize a lot of big, impressive words to use it. You already know all the words you need to coin power phrases. You just need to learn a special trick for putting the words you do know together in a whole new way.

If you are writing, power phrases are your best friends when it comes to memos, reports, speeches, newsletter articles, important letters, and resumes. If you are speaking, power phrases are your best friend, whether it's expressing yourself in casual conversation, explaining your department's efforts at a meeting, introducing someone at a banquet, giving a speech, or conducting a workshop. Whatever the circumstance, developing the knack of putting words together so that they are both interesting and state your position clearly will be a major step forward in raising your verbal intelligence.

THE POWER OF WORDS

It is said, "One picture is worth a thousand words." But no picture ever started a war, or brought about a peace, or liberated a people, or started a new religion. Clearly, words are worth far more than the most impressive painting, and the pen is mightier than the mightiest sword. Charles Dickens knew this when he penned *A Christmas Carol* and slipped in his satiric barbs against the Victorian practice of sending the poor and old people to workhouses, where they were forced to tread in a circle ten hours a day turning a millwheel. Rachel Carson knew it when she wrote *Silent Spring*, the book that put ecological awareness on the map. Alex Haley knew it when he published his immortal *Roots* and roused a people to reclaim a shattered heritage.

When you think about great advertising campaigns, is it a picture you remember or the "jingle"? Chances are you can instantly identify the product associated with all these: "Have it your way." "They'rrrr grrrrreat!" "It's the real thing." "We try harder."

A great man, being overly modest, mistakenly thought the world would little note nor long remember what he said one bright spring afternoon. He believed it was the events he and others had gathered to commemorate that would echo down through history. Instead, about the only Civil War battlefield most people can remember is Gettysburg, and they remember it, not because of the valiant sacrifices made there in 1863, but because its name is featured in the title of the single most famous speech in American history.

That's the power of well-written words!

POWER PHRASES: WORDS THAT MOVE AND MOTIVATE

The fact that some phrases have a unique capacity all their own to move and motivate people was discovered by linguists in the early part of this century. But the secret of coining power phrases has remained virtually unknown outside a small clique of psychologists and linguists who have studied them. The few experts who have written about them have called them "high-performance phrases," "sizzlers," "wake-ups," "grabbers," and "power words."

But I prefer the term "power phrases." I feel this more accurately reflects what they are because "power" suggests the impact and force with which they can strike others and because "phrases" reflects the fact that words are never used alone, but always in combination.

Power phrases are particularly valuable when you are trying to motivate others to take a specific action. Politicians have always used power phrases to mobilize a citizenry and enlist their efforts in a cause. Just consider these memorable gems: "We have nothing to fear but fear itself"; "Ask not what your country can do for you, but what you can do for your country."

Advertising is another fount of unforgettable power phrases that have moved millions to think of one particular product when they want a soft drink, or a can of soup, or a washday detergent. Writers often use them to conclude books on a memorable note. You can probably identify the novels most of these come from: "Tomorrow is another day." "God bless us, every one." "Isn't it pretty to think so." (In order, they are *Gone with the Wind*, *A Christmas Carol*, and *The Sun Also Rises.*)

SIX STEPS TO POWER WRITING

What makes a phrase a "power phrase"? A power phrase is a vivid combination of two or more words (though most are no longer than four) that conveys its meaning instantly and stands out so powerfully from other words that it makes an immediate impact on a reader's or listener's mind. Phrases gain power when they share at least three of the following qualities. (I call them the six criteria of a power phrase.) You know you have coined a power phrase when it

1. Is dramatic and vivid

2. Is easily pictured or understood

3. Makes a bold statement

4. Contains important information or a call to action

5. Piques interest

6. Is concise and succinct

When the phrases you coin are easily pictured by other people, relate to their personal experiences, and offer something they want, you've got a winner. Once you have acquired the knack, you can draw on your ability to create power phrases to help compel attention and make your point forcefully in every kind of situation. People will pay close heed to what you have to say and write and will feel impelled into action by your choice of words.

COINING POWER PHRASES

Coming up with vivid, exciting combinations of words that impress your thoughts on others probably feels daunting. Coining power phrases might seem as if it is something that would require special genius—or hours of labor at the least. Nothing could be further from the truth. Anyone can generate power phrases using this simple, six-step exercise, and the entire process takes less than fifteen minutes. That's because it draws on a hidden genius for words you already possess. The six steps are:

1. State what you want to say in your own words.
2. Restate it with a strong, positive spin.
3. Generate several more positive restatements.
4. Underline the most powerful words you've produced.
5. Combine the underlined words creatively.
6. Compare your results with the six criteria in the preceding section.

This may sound too easy, but it's merely a slightly simplified version of the same process writers and advertising copywriters use (often unconsciously) to create blockbuster prose and unforgettable ad lines.

VERBAL INTELLIGENCE BUILDER: POWER PHRASES

Here is how you might use this six-step exercise to coin power phrases in real life: Say you work in the control department of an aircraft manufacturing corporation. The number of faulty parts that have gotten past your inspectors has gone up. Management has asked you to come up with a remedy.

After some weeks of thought you devise a program that you think will reduce errors almost to zero. But you are realistic enough to know that the program itself is worthless unless you can mobilize everyone involved to stand behind it. To do that, you know you will need some kind of catchphrase that will encapsulate the program with a strong verbal punch.

Before, you would have make the mistake of settling for a commonplace phrase such as, "A Plan for Reducing Quality Control Errors." But now that you have learned about power phrases, you know it's possible to do better. You decide to take the extra few minutes and apply what you know about coining power phrases to the problem. Take out a sheet of blank paper (or open up a new computer file). Here is how you might proceed:

1. *Write down what you want to say in your own words.* Hint: Set down the first words that come to mind (it doesn't matter how awkward or inadequate they feel). You might write something like "reduce the errors my department is making to zero and eliminate defects."

2. *Rephrase what you have written to give it as positive a spin as possible.* For example, "Get it 100 percent right."

3. *Using what you have just written as inspiration, dream up four or five other positive ways you might formulate your point.* You might write, "Get more quality in quality control," and "No tolerance for errors."

4. *Go over everything you have written, including your first, rough try at what you wanted to say.* Underline or put a check mark next to the words you think have the most power (unless something you have written already looks like an ideal candidate for a power phrase; in which case, skip the next two steps and go straight to the checklist that follows). For example, you might well underline the following in the phrases you wrote: "Reduce the errors my department is making to <u>zero</u> and eliminate <u>defects</u>." "Get it <u>100 percent right</u>"; "Get more <u>quality in quality control</u>," and "No <u>tolerance</u> for errors."

5. *Try putting the words you have underlined together in different creative combinations.* Write down the results. You might end up with phrases like, "100 percent quality," "zero tolerance," "control defects," "zero tolerance for defects," "adding the quality to quality control," "control quality, zero defects," or "100 percent quality, 100 percent of the time," and so forth.

6. *Pick several possibilities, compare them with the six criteria for a power phrase* (dramatic and vivid, easily pictured or understood, makes a bold statement, important information or a call to action, peaks interest, concise and succinct).

If you are still dissatisfied with what you have produced and don't feel any are worth checking, set what you have written aside and begin over again. Almost everyone who tries this process reports they come up with something useful the second time through.

How Power Phrases Helped A Real Estate Agent Double Her Business

In his book, *How to Be Twice as Smart,* performance consultant Scott Witt says there is no better test of the impact power phrases can have than apartment ads in a newspaper. People who are looking for apartments have a lot of small ads with tiny type to scan. Most contain a short, unimaginative headline in boldface, intended to catch the aspiring apartment hunter's attention. Stock headlines include, "Spacious one-bedroom," "Close to shopping," "Charming patio."

The one quality these headlines share is a lack of excitement; even the adjectives "spacious", "charming," or "view" are such long-standing real estate ad clichés as to rate only a "ho-hum." You might even think there'd not be much opportunity for a power phrase there. But one apartment agent, Wendy, took a different point of view.

Wendy had learned about power phrases from Witt, who calls them "high-performance words." Wendy decided that rather than headlines that reflected the standard elements of apartments—number of bedrooms, size, location—her headlines would focus instead on what was unique (pique interest). She decided it didn't matter how other real estate agents had been writing ads, since she was writing hers for prospective tenants, not for her fellow professionals.

To create her headlines, Wendy used the same technique for generating power phrases contained in today's exercise. The results speak for themselves. According to Wendy her business doubled within six months, and she became the most sought-after rental agent in town, with property owners clamoring to become clients.

SIMPLE WORDS, POWERFUL RESULTS

Though they produced amazing effects, the headlines Wendy coined didn't rely on fancy language. Instead, they all put simple everyday words together to announce attractive qualities no one seeking an apartment could resist.

Here are a few samples:

Safe Neighborhood

Free Electricity

Kids Welcome

Friendly Neighbors

Watch the Ships Come In

Cats, Dogs, Goldfish OK

These headlines are so simple they may not look like power phrases to you at first. But if you pause and reflect on them more carefully, you will see just why they qualify. What you'll learn will help spark your writing in many ways, even if you never have to write a classified ad.

1. *Dramatic and vivid.* At least three of these headlines fit this criterion. "Safe Neighborhood" and "Free Electricity" both reach out and grab you, while "Watch the Ships Come In" has the vividness of a photograph.

2. *Easily pictured or understood.* All the headlines draw on the same everyday language we all use. "Electricity" and "Neighbors" are the biggest words used.

3. *Makes a bold statement.* Considering how many apartment houses today prohibit children, "Kids Welcome" is a bold statement certain to catch any parent's attention. So is the announcement that you will be "safe" if you move into one apartment, or that you will be welcomed by "friendly neighbors" if you rent the other.

4. *Contains important information or a call to action.* Consider the following facts: you don't have to pay for electricity; this apartment house takes families; you have an ocean view.

5. *Piques interest.* Who can resist something's that's "free," and in times where crime and violence seem endemic, who doesn't long to live in a "safe neighborhood"?

6. *Concise and succinct.* None of Wendy's headlines were longer than five words; most were only two words. But each compelled attention.

Creating power phrases may sound as if it would be cumbersome and take an undue length of time, but it's a skill, just like typing, that improves with exercise. The more you do it, the faster and easier it becomes.

THE POWER TECHNIQUE YOU'LL LEARN TOMORROW

With the success of developing your writing skills behind you, tomorrow's exercise will propel you further toward super brain power, guiding you through a strategy so dynamic that it can transform even the most tongue-tied individual into a good conversationalist and a well-liked public speaker.

DAY 2 —————————————————————————

EXERCISE: POWER SPEAKING

Today's exercise will enable you to build up a second aspect of your verbal intelligence, as you learn the ultimate insider trick for making yourself a speaking success.

The skill you learn won't require any special dramatic ability or linguistic talent on your part. You don't have to learn how to write and deliver speeches, or memorize complicated conversational gambits to help you interact smoothly with others. Again, you simply unlock the hidden genius of your verbal intelligence.

This technique, which I call "power speaking," is so potent it will turn even the most tongue-tied wallflower into an engaging conversationalist and a speaker who can stir interest in even the most routine topics. You will have the power to walk confidently into parties or high-stakes business meetings and have your say in a way everyone respects.

Better yet, if you can order a cup of coffee in a restaurant, you already possess the number-one skill it takes to learn "power speaking."

WHY YOU CAN ALREADY TALK AS WELL AS YOU NEED TO—AND DON'T KNOW IT

The power speaking exercise that follows will raise your verbal intelligence by developing your native ability to talk clearly, coherently, convincingly to and before others. That claim may seem to take in a great deal of territory. It may even sound intimidating if you are someone who has always had difficulty expressing him or herself before others, whether it's at a social gathering or a department meeting.

But consider this: You learned to make yourself understood (and to understand) in English, which scholars worldwide rate as one of the most difficult languages to master. After all, you talk to people, make yourself perfectly clear, and get the results you want dozens of times every day. You can order a cup of coffee at a donut shop, ask your spouse to pass the butter, tell your eight-year-old it's time for bed, or even request a coworker to hand you a stapler.

In short, you can make yourself understood as well as anyone in routine, everyday interactions with others. There's no pressure on, no one judging you, and you vocalize your thoughts offhand, without especially thinking about it—unselfconsciously.

If you are like most people, what misleads you into believing you are a poor conversationalist and speaker is that you freeze up and become tongue-tied when the situation is less casual, when you know others will be forming their opinions of you based on the ideas and opinions you express and how well you express them. You then base your estimation of your speaking skills on how well you come off in these situations—and conclude that it is quite low.

In other words, you don't have a problem with talking to other people at all, as long as you are not particularly thinking about it.

THE THREE SLAYERS OF SPEAKING SELF-CONFIDENCE

It's only in circumstances that cause you to become self-conscious about how clearly and intelligently you are speaking that you have a problem with verbalizing your thoughts. If you are at all uncertain about your skill at verbalizing yourself, then there are three kinds of situations where you are likely to find yourself less than articulate.

Conversational confidence usually evaporates when people find themselves facing

- Social gatherings
- Business meetings
- Making speeches

If you have the slightest tendency toward social shyness, then whenever you find yourself in one of these three situations you probably begin by worrying about how well you are getting your ideas across and end by second-guessing what you are saying as you say it. Was that remark good enough? Is there any way it could offend anyone? Is there a better way to phrase it?

Naturally, you stumble over your own words, changing your mind a half-dozen times in midstream, and what you say comes out in a jumble (an amalgam of all those half-articulated versions of words you were trying to decide between). Or you simply decide silence is the safest course and stand there like a bump on a log, feeling awkward and ill at ease and wishing you were at home instead.

You are like the sleepwalker who is walking obliviously along the ledge of a balcony with perfect balance. If suddenly brought out of the trance and made aware of his precarious predicament, the sleepwalker can become so nervous he loses his balance and falls off.

Fortunately, there is a simple way out of this box. Follow the example of a man who tapped his hidden verbal genius and became a beloved world figure.

HOW TO BECOME A POPULAR SPEAKER, NO MATTER HOW TONGUE-TIED YOU ARE

He spoke slowly, had a backwoods drawl, everything he said sounded as if he had just come off the farm, and his voice had a monotonous, nasal quality. But he went on to become one of the most successful speakers, actors, and writers of the early twentieth century. He was the great folk humorist Will Rogers, and once people got past his delivery to his wry, satirical comments on American institutions and figures, they laughed and loved him and kept on coming back for more. (Mark Russell, hardly the world's greatest singer, is a contemporary example.)

Rogers was the first to acknowledge that he didn't do anything special to earn his success. "Why back home they say, 'Will's just talking the way he used to on the street corner around here. Old Cap Stallings can talk better than that.'"

What did Will Rogers know that you don't know? What was the secret of his amazing success?

Rogers had stumbled on what public speaking mavens such as Tony Robbins and Marianne Williamson agree is the number-one secret of speaking mastery.

Is it a way of speaking? A trick for putting words together? A special way of presenting your material?

No, it's nothing as complicated as that. The key trick of public speaking mastery is simply . . . to be yourself. All the experts agree, whether it's an anniversary party for a neighbor or a talk about your department's final plan for expanded growth in the twenty-first century, your best likelihood of making a hit is to "act natural." Say the things you have to say the way you would say them if you were standing in the shower or lounging in the bath talking to yourself.

That's what Will Rogers did, and here are some of the pearls that resulted: "They're as busy as usual in Congress passing appropriations bills like hot biscuits at a country farmhouse." "Americans will join anything in town but their own families." "There ain't but one word wrong with every one of us in the world and that word is self-ishness." "Congressional investigations are for the benefit of the photographers." "In the early days of the U.S., we had no churches. Now we got plenty of churches, and no congregations."

VERBAL INTELLIGENCE BUILDER: POWER SPEAKING

Of course, it's not easy acting naturally if you feel self-conscious and awkward, that all eyes are upon you. But the following exercise will lead you through six surefire steps for unlocking the hidden genius of being yourself in the face of any conversational or speaking challenge. Next time you find yourself facing a social occasion or company meeting or you need to make a speech, keep the following simple rules in mind.

1. *DO talk normally.* Give your natural voice and intonations their freedom. Don't try to hide accents, gravely voices, regional twangs or drawls, and other unique aspects of the way you typically speak. Studies show people are both fascinated and intimidated by those with unusual accents. An accent suggests someone of a different background with wider experiences who might know more about life than we do. And consider this: From Katharine Hepburn to Goldie Hawn, from Paul Harvey to Rush Limbaugh, the actors and announcers who become megasuccesses all have some unique quality to their voice that made them stand out from others. What this means is that an accent or distinctive manner of speaking works in your favor, not against you. People give what you say more weight, and what you say sounds wiser. The best news is that even when you *do* slip and say something dumb, it will actually sound more intelligent because of your accent. You can relax and be more confident, because you know your accent is doing half the work of making your points for you. So you don't have to strain so hard or worry so much about whether you are expressing yourself as well as you would like.

2. *DO reflect your background in the way you speak.* Every profession, business, sport, and hobby has its own insider lingo—special words, phrases, and figures of speech used only by members of that particular fraternity and that are mostly unknown to outsiders. If you are a rancher, giving a presentation before an Eastern meat-packing firm, salt what you have to say with the kind of phrases you and your friends typically use when talking to each other. You might complain that something was "harder than winter mud" or "colder than a bureaucrat's smile." Your profession or hobby group, even your church, has a few of its own patented phrases. You may not be aware of this, because you are constantly surrounded by others who talk the same way. When legendary writer/producer/director/star Jack Webb was creating *Dragnet*, the authentic police drama that has become a cultural icon, he spent several weeks riding with police detectives on their nightly rounds. Webb told the two officers he wanted to learn everything he could about "police jargon" and how detectives talked on the job. "We don't talk any different than you do," one surprised policeman protested. But when Webb asked the detective what he'd do if he had a serious suspect in a case, the officer replied that, "I'd go down to 'R and I' [records and identification] and pull the package [suspect's records]." An excited Webb exclaimed, "That's it. That's what I mean. Police lingo!" Take a lesson from Webb's success, slip a few colorful insider phrases from your profession or hobby into what you have to say now and then. Insider lingo like this confers additional power on even the weakest presentation by making your listeners feel they are privileged insiders being let in on trade secrets (which in a sense they are). They listen more carefully to what you are saying in the hopes of hearing another such priceless jewel.

3. *DO stick to what you know.* By focusing on your areas of expertise, you will speak with greater confidence and clarity. People will sense your authority and pay closer attention to what you are saying, whether or not they consider your presentation spellbinding.

4. *DO admit you don't know the answer.* If someone asks you a question you can't honestly answer, don't attempt to bluff or pretend you know. You will only be caught out at some point by somebody, be revealed as a person whose statements can't be trusted at face value, and lose your credibility with everyone involved. It's better to confess your ignorance of the matter and promise you will check into the subject and learn the answer. This makes you seem like someone who is both honest and willing to learn, and people will respect you for it (and if you keep your word and do the research, they'll respect you even more).

5. *DO let your passion for your subject show.* You don't have to overdo it by trying to convert everyone to your subject, or by remaining at a fever pitch that overpowers your listeners and leaves them no chance to respond. But let your enthusiasm, your passion, your interest, your anger, and, yes, your amusement show—if that is what you are feeling. World-class speakers say there's more than a grain of truth in the old adage that enthusiasm is contagious. No matter how dry or plain the topic, if the person speaking suggests by her or his manner that it is a subject of great interest, others will listen more closely, waiting to find out why.

THE POWER TECHNIQUE YOU'LL LEARN TOMORROW

Having built your verbal IQ higher than you imagined possible with the power writing and power speaking techniques, tomorrow you will raise it even higher. You will learn the secret of transforming your current listening skills into the ability to pick out the exact information you want from any conversation, lecture, or workshop and lock it into your memory, forever.

EXERCISE: LASER-GUIDED LISTENING

Today you are going to learn how to become a better listener than Sigmund Freud, Johnny Carson, or Barbara Walters. As with the other exercises in this program, power listening will strengthen your verbal IQ by drawing on and expanding your natural ability to hear and understand words.

Listening might not sound like a key building block on the road to success, a key to super brain power compared to writing and speaking, but success experts rate it an essential for personal and professional advancement. "Effective listening projects as much personal power as speaking," writes Dr. Florence Seaman in *Winning at Work*. "Make sure that you have the time to listen, then pay attention to the person, look at him, listen to the content of what he is saying."

Perhaps the value of good listening skills shouldn't be surprising. More than 78 percent of the information we take in on an average day is presented in the form of the spoken word. Supervisors summon us in to explain a new project, the television weatherperson announces the day's forecast, a spouse details the complex new work schedule he'll have to maintain for a month, the loan officer phones to describe additional documentation she will need to process your application, the stylist describes a new idea for cutting your hair.

Yet oddly, for all its significance, listening is the one skill taught by no grade, middle, high school, college or university. Surveys show up to 98 percent of the population cannot name even three basic principles of good listening. Perhaps it's not so strange, then, that those same surveys also reveal that while we tend to underestimate our capability for writing and speaking, we tend to overestimate our competency as listeners.

HOW A PUBLISHER DISCOVERED THE POWER OF LISTENING

Arkady owned a publishing company that specialized in distributing expensive, lavishly illustrated directories of local events, restaurants, attractions, and recreations to hotels in major cities throughout the South. All the printing was done at a plant Arkady owned in Atlanta, with cover photographs, advertisements, and listings sent in from some two dozen editorial and design staffs in the cities where the guides were distributed. Each week Arkady split his time among his home office, the printing plant, and his far-flung editorial operations. He spent two days each at his office and the plant, and flew into a different city each Friday for an all-day conference with his staff there.

Needless to say, since his employees had access to Arkady in person only a small portion of each week, they besieged him with meetings, reports, questions, and urgent problems to be solved during the time he spent with them. Interruptions to beseech his counsel on some critical matter were so frequent that sometimes Arkady found himself with three and four people talking with him at the same time. The result was auditory and verbal overload.

Arkady felt himself beginning to experience burnout trying to take in everything everyone was saying to him—sometimes all at once. Arkady detailed these woes to a mutual friend one day. She brought the two of us together.

I explained to Arkady that his dilemma was in part caused by the belief that there is only one kind of listening, and that was to try and hear every word everyone says—a wonderful approach if you are alone with another person or listening to an unusually interesting speech, but not always practical in every situation.

Instead, I told Arkady that there are five stages of normal listening, each with its unique benefits and drawbacks. Simply by using the level of listening appropriate to the person or situation, Arkady could significantly reduce his state of aural overload.

The five stages, as I described them to Arkady, are

1. Not really listening

2. Barely listening

3. Selective listening

4. Attentive listening

5. Empathetic listening

In addition, I informed Arkady, there is a sixth stage of listening, power listening, that incorporates all the best features of the other five.

HOW TO USE THE FIVE LEVELS OF LISTENING POWER

You have probably used every one of the five levels of listening before. What you may not have done is stop to analyze the process, break it down into separate levels, and consider the benefits and drawbacks of each. But once you do, merely by using each consciously, in the right circumstances, you can measurably raise both your listening power and your verbal IQ (not to mention save yourself from "auditory burnout").

1. *Not really listening.* We sometimes call this "stonewalling," "tuning the other person out," or "turning a deaf ear." You let the other person talk, but don't pay attention to what he or she is saying. Great for when you can't shut someone up and simply must focus on something else. Downside is that you might miss something truly meaningful.

2. *Barely listening.* We sometimes call this "listening for cues" and "pretending to listen." All you actually listen for are the pauses (or) cues that indicate the other person has stopped and is waiting for a response, so that you can interject an "UMMM-humm" or "tell me more" that implies you are listening and then go back to your own thoughts. Great for tuning people out, when you feel you must, without offending them. Downside again is that you may fail to catch crucial information.

3. *Selective listening.* We sometimes call this "listening for what's in it for us." You keep a mental antenna out for anything the other person says that might be of personal interest to you, but you don't hear the rest. Great when you don't want to block out anything important, but do want to screen out "old news." Downside is you still run the risk of not hearing something critical because it lacks the right cue words or because you are concentrating too hard on something else.

4. *Attentive listening.* We sometimes call this "focused listening," "active listening," and "paying attention." You concentrate all your listening powers on what the other person is saying. Great when the subject is crucial or the presentation is dense with facts and insights. Downside is that much of the effort is wasted, as studies show up to 90 percent of what even the best speakers have to say is made up of words such as "but," "and," "of," and "therefore" that convey absolutely no information.

5. *Empathetic listening.* We sometimes call this "listening from inside out" and "intuitive listening." You attempt to go beyond merely hearing the other person's words and attempt to place yourself inside his or her mind and see what the person is saying and why the person is saying it from his or her perspective. Good when you are trying to understand why someone else sees things so differently from the way you do or when you want to resolve disputes and disagreements. Downside is that no one can truly know the inside of another person's mind, which can be the cause of further misunderstanding, as well as the enormous energy drain listening of this kind takes.

THE SIXTH LEVEL OF LISTENING: POWER LISTENING

Although each of the preceding five levels has its advantages, all possess some degree of disadvantage. But there is a sixth approach to listening. It has all the pluses of the first five and none of their minuses. I call it power listening. Some people have described its effect as being a lot like "growing an extra set of ears."

Power listening will enable you to

- Remember key facts and figures, even when they are reeled off impromptu at a conference

- Extract all the essentials from a long boring speech without having to torture your ears listening to every word

* Strain out extraneous, repetitious, boring material, while bringing you to instant attention at the slightest mention of anything important to you

VERBAL INTELLIGENCE BUILDER: FOUR STEPS TO POWER LISTENING

This four-step exercise will unlock your verbal IQ by giving you laser-guided hearing that ignores unimportant "filler" and distraction, while locking in on and extracting only the parts you need to hear. For instance, Colby found himself suddenly faced with making a critical decision overnight, on the same evening he was scheduled to attend an Anthony Robbins seminar for which he had already paid more than fifteen hundred dollars. Using power listening, he was able to tune out everything he already knew, while coming instantly alert the moment a new technique or principle was introduced. Meanwhile, he was able to mull over all the aspects of the decision he had to make, during the portions of the presentation that were "old news" to him.

Another of my students, Adrienne, worked in a marketing firm where bullpen discussions were often fast and furious, with everyone so excited they were often all talking at once. She felt as if she were missing "at least half of what's being said." But with the power-listening technique she was able to follow and pinpoint the essentials, no matter how many of her vociferous colleagues were talking over each other.

1. *Listen carefully for summaries at the beginning and end.* At the start of most speeches, lectures, seminars, and even audiotapes, the speaker gives a rundown of his or her basic topic and its subtopics. Tune in completely at the beginning to find out if the speaker's key ideas are previewed there. If not, tune back into the speaker at the end. You'll probably hear a summary there.

2. *Listen for key words.* Keep half an ear out for key words that are likely to appear in any discussion of the topics and subtopics that will contain the information of greatest interest to you. Any time you hear one, redirect your full attention to the speaker until you determine whether what is being said is relevant to your own needs. If it isn't, tune back out. But if it is relevant, keep listening until there is another change of subject, or until the speaker drifts to extraneous material again.

3. *Listen for "change-of-pace" words that signal a new topic is about to be introduced.* In English, certain words have come to be conventions used for alerting audiences that the speaker is about to change the subject. Once you have gleaned the basics of what a speaker has to say on one topic, you can tune out until you hear one of these words. The "change-of-pace" words include "now," "moving on," "but," "next," "thus," "therefore," "in addition," "a good method," "a different approach."

4. *Ignore details.* Some details you need to know, of course. But, often the details consist of anecdotes or additional statistics designed to support ideas the speaker has presented. If it's the ideas you are after, you can safely skip all the material piled on solely to corroborate the main thesis. Even if you are interested in what evidence there is to support the speaker's contention, tuning in on just a couple will do, and once you think you can follow the speaker's reasoning, you can tune out again.

To wring the maximum benefit from power listening, make use of the "mental downtime," when the speaker is droning on with irrelevant material, to review and stick in your memory anything of significance you have already heard.

THE POWER TECHNIQUE YOU'LL LEARN TOMORROW

The final verbal intelligence builder will show you how to unlock super brain power by zipping through reports, manuals, and research books twice as fast—with twice the comprehension. But this amazing technique won't stop there. It has turned thousands of reading-haters into reading-likers. (If you are one, you'll probably be surprised to discover yourself becoming a reading-lover too. But, I thought you might be more willing to believe it might be possible to "like" reading.)

Day 4 —————————————————————————————

EXERCISE: SUPER-READING

The fourth day of the super brain power program, and the last devoted to verbal IQ, will bolster your word smarts by liberating the natural speed-reader inside you. Left to itself, your verbal intelligence will zip through books, reports, memos, manuals, newspapers, and magazines in record time. This technique will also transform any reluctance you feel toward reading into an actual hunger for the writer's words.

Reading has been left until last to show you that you can raise your verbal IQ through writing, speaking, and listening. If you were someone who doesn't read, or you thought you didn't like reading, and if the reading section had come first, you probably wouldn't have believed the assertion that the power reading exercise can inculcate a genuine love of reading. You might even have been tempted to skip it entirely. But, having experienced the benefits of the initial three exercises, you will be more likely to stick with it, giving the power reading exercise a chance.

The eye and the brain can absorb hundreds of words per minute. But, we typically read much more slowly. Why? Because we unconsciously inhibit our verbal intelligence's innate gifts for reading. By the end of today, you will have freed your hidden genius from these shackles and will be well on the way to becoming the speed reader you were meant to be.

HOW ELENA WENT FROM READING-HATER TO READING-LIKER IN ONE SESSION

Elena's career seemed to be stuck in the lower echelons of management for a large software manufacturer. Bright, capable, with excellent interpersonal skills, Elena had to sit silently and watch while the promotions went to men and women less capable than herself. For Elena had only a BA, and the passkey to upper management in her company was an MBA.

Elena's immediate supervisors recognized her potential and even encouraged her to go for that missing MBA. They dangled the company's support, flextime, financial aid, even special tutoring if she needed it. Elena was always flattered, always agreed she wanted to return to college and earn an MBA, but always found a reason for putting it off.

Finally, Elena came to me in tears and confessed the secret that had held her back. "Could you teach me speed-reading," she wailed. "I'm the world's slowest reader, and I always seem to have to go back over everything three or four times to understand it. In fact, I hate reading, and have ever since grade school. I've never even finished an entire book in my life. I managed to scrape through to my BA only by taking copious notes during classes. But an MBA program involves so much reading that I could never fake my way through on note-taking alone. But, if I could speed-read through all those books . . ."

WHY YOU READ SLOWLY AND WHAT YOU CAN DO ABOUT IT

Elena was suffering from a common misconception. She had her cart before her horse. Like many people who read ploddingly and look on it as a chore, she thought she disliked reading because she read so slowly. The truth, that people read slowly because they dislike reading had never occurred to her.

I told Elena that I was going to share the most effective speed-reading technique of all. It was the same technique that enabled the world's most celebrated readers—people such as Isaac Asimov, William F. Buckley, and Barbara Walters—to read their way through so many books. But, instead of focusing on externals such as sweeping the eyes in zigzag patterns or timed readings, this strategy would boast her verbal IQ and multiply her reading speed, beginning from the inside out.

In fact, I promised a doubting Elena that this strategy was so powerful it would transform her strong antipathy for reading the first time she tried it.

Elena didn't believe me at the time. But I assured her that thousands of people I've worked with have used these techniques to turn around their entire attitude toward reading. They have gone from an overwhelming negative to an overwhelming positive—and in a single session. I promised to teach Elena what some people called speed-reading techniques later, if she wanted.

But, first, I asked her to trust me and try the technique I had mentioned, a method for becoming so engrossed in what you are reading that you automatically begin reading more quickly just to find out more. I told her I call this exercise "power reading" and that it is very easy to learn. It follows here. Elena phoned two days later to announce that it had, indeed, transformed her attitude toward books. "I actually read a fascinating article this morning in the newspaper," she announced proudly. "I guess I'll give that MBA a whirl, after all."

VERBAL INTELLIGENCE BUILDER: POWER READING

This exercise will save you hours of reading time and transform any antipathy you feel toward reading into total involvement. You may start as a book-hater, but you will end as a book-liker who can use more of your verbal intelligence more of the time.

In fact, this exercise is especially designed with those who hate reading. You don't even have to do any real reading. All you have to do is to be able to skim, and as someone once said about putting two lips together to whistle, you do know how to do that, don't you?

You will need writing material and a nonfiction book that you haven't already read. The book should be on a subject of interest to you. Business or hobbies are especially recommended for this particular exercise, as the subject will hold a natural interest and will be more likely to hold you reading once you get started.

Your book must have

- A short summary or overview of its subject, along with a brief biography of the author, on a dust jacket or back cover

- A table of contents giving the title of each chapter

- An Introduction, Preface, or Foreword by the author

- A subject index at the end

- Frequent headings, in capital letters or boldfaced, summarizing the content of the material that follows

This exercise is in two parts, but it won't take more than half an hour. That isn't too much to gamble on coming out a more committed reader, is it? And, admit it, even if you detest reading, you have wasted half an hour before watching a terrible television sitcom, haven't you? Isn't learning to become a power reader worth at least the same investment?

PART A

1. Skim the back cover or dust jacket to discover what the publisher has to say about your book.

2. Skim the description of the author's background and areas of expertise.

3. Skim the table of contents and see how the author has organized the information into parts, chapters, or other subsections.

4. Skim whatever opening material contains the author's personal overview of the book (usually found in the Introduction or Foreword or Preface).

5. Skim the headings only, starting with Chapter One and working your way toward the end of the book. (If any of the subjects particularly catches your eye and seems interesting, it's okay to stop and skim a couple of paragraphs, just to satisfy your curiosity.)

PART B

1. On a sheet of paper (or in a computer file) write the following phrase: "Skimming the book this way, made me curious about . . . ," and then list two questions you had about what you skimmed. (You can list more, if you want, but be sure to list at least two.)

2. Next, write, "Skimming the book this way, I learned . . . ," and then list anything new you spotted that you didn't know before.

3. Next, write, "Skimming the book this way, I was bored by . . . ," and then list any subjects that especially turned you off.

4. Next, write, "Skimming the book this way, my attention was caught by . . . ," and then list whatever ideas or topics interested, excited, or intrigued you.

5. Now, pause for a moment and check in with yourself. You may be surprised to discover yourself feeling a bit differently toward this book than you normally do toward one you've attempted to read the old-fashioned way. Heightened curiosity and interest are typical reactions, along with a more personal sense of connection with the book and deeper satisfaction in owning it as a valuable informational resource.

6. Finally, use the book to find the answers to the questions you listed during Step 1. Beginning with the first question, turn to the index in the back of the book. Look up the subject of your curiosity in the index. You will see one or more page numbers following the word you have looked up. Write these down; they are the pages where references to your topic can found. Skim through these pages until you find the one that answers your questions and satisfies your curiosity. (If you can't locate your subject under the first word you think of, don't give up—try a synonym. Every topic covered in the book is likely to be indexed; it's just a matter of finding the way they've listed it.)

Using this system, go through the book over the next few days until you feel you have found out everything that could be of use or interest to you.

Beginning your reading of a book or manual or report like this, with a clear idea of what questions you already have about the subject it can answer, may not seem like much of a step. But, it is literally a whole new way of reading if you aren't a book-lover. It supplies the missing ingredient that makes people love reading: a personal stake in what they are about to read.

You can prove this for yourself. Pause for a moment after performing the preceding exercise. Ask yourself these questions: Do you feel differently about getting started on the book from the way you usually feel? Did you experience more interest, possibly even excitement, as you discovered answers to your questions? Is there any difference in the quality of the information you have gained?

If the answers to the preceding are yes, you have just raised your verbal IQ and joined the legions of book-likers.

LIBERATING YOUR INNER READER FROM THE THREE READING-WRECKERS

After developing a taste for reading, the first thing most people want to know is how they can read faster. Their thoughts turn naturally, as Elena's did, to speed-reading courses and books. But, as noted earlier, you don't have to learn any special tricks or techniques to be able to read faster. Your innate verbal intelligence *is* already a speed-reader. All you need to do is get out of its way, and left to its own, your "inner reader" will sail through pages of type with complete comprehension at simply amazing rates.

The secret is to free yourself from three bad reading habits that typically shackle the brain's natural reading capacities. These "reading-wreckers" are ways of reading so counterproductive they can even retard the verbal IQ of a reading-lover.

You free your verbal intelligence to reach its own natural reading speed when you avoid these three reading-wreckers:

- DON'T follow words with your fingers or move your head.
- DON'T sound out words, or move your lips.
- DON'T go back and reread what you've already read once.

Keep these rules in mind as you read, and you will find yourself reading farther, faster, and with a lessened sense of strain.

THE POWER TECHNIQUE YOU WILL
LEARN TOMORROW

At this point, you are well on your way toward unlocking the six keys to your hidden genius. And you know the exercises in this program work. With tomorrow's exercise you will begin the first of the three days devoted to the second key: your visual intelligence.

The Second Key—

UNLOCKING YOUR VISUAL GENIUS

WHAT'S YOUR
VISUAL
IQ?

Like the self-assessment quiz for verbal intelligence, this test will enable you to rate the current state of your visual intelligence. Whatever your score, beginning with today's exercise, you can raise your picture smarts if they seem in need of expansion. Or you can take an already high visual IQ and blow it right through the top of the chart.

Check the box beside any description that feels as if it applies to you.

☑ Do you experience vivid, detailed daydreams and night dreams?

☑ Do you like to draw or doodle?

☐ Do you seldom spend a day without stopping to notice something beautiful in your surroundings: a gorgeous sky, a beautiful flower, a vivid picture?

☑ Do you see pictures and images when you think, rather than hearing words in your head?

☐ Are a do-it-yourselfer, always tinkering with machines, cars, appliances?

☑ Are you fascinated by how things work?

☐ Do you easily recall the exact size and shapes of objects?

☑ Do you like to study information on posters, charts, and graphics?

☑ Do you pick up instantly on visual clues?

☐ Did you spend hours playing with Legos, erector sets, and three-dimensional puzzles as a kid?

☑ Do you picture events and people when you hear them described in a conversation or report?

☐ Do you rarely get lost?

☑ Are you keenly aware of color?

☐ Do you like to relax by doing jigsaw puzzles, mazes, optical illusions, and other visual puzzles?

☐ Was geometry easier than algebra in school?

☐ Can you comfortably imagine how something might appear if it were looked down upon from directly above in a bird's-eye view?

☐ Do you like to arrange the slides you took on vacation into a little show, use a camcorder to shoot videotapes of family gatherings, maintain an album filled with photos of those near and dear to you?

☐ Do you create charts and graphs for business presentations?

☑ Do you like to tour art galleries and museums, or watch videos and movies?

☑ Do you read colorful newspapers such as *USA Today* and page through heavily illustrated magazines such as *Vanity Fair, Sports Illustrated, National Geographic,* and *People?*

☐ Do you do crossword puzzles?

Scoring: Add up the number of boxes you checked.

If your score was between 1 and 4, you are in serious need of today's exercise. Your visual intelligence is about to atrophy from neglect. Put it on a daily workout program, and you will be surprised at the results even a few days can make.

If your score was between 5 and 12, you may appreciate a beautiful sunset or a well-photographed movie, but your image smarts are primarily a passive thing. You have them, but don't use them much.

However, the three days focused on visual IQ will give you such a strong taste of its potential for helping you toward success that you will want to develop all its capacities. If your score was between 13 and 17, your hobby could be painting, visiting museums, or posting cool graphics on your webpage. You stand out in picture smarts, and with a bit of exercise could lift your visual IQ to the genius class.

If your score was between 18 and 20, you are at the top of the class! Your profession involves art, advertising, craftsmanship, or something that fully engages your visual talents. The exercises that follow won't tax visual intelligence in your range, but you'll probably find yourself responding to the challenge and wanting to do them anyway.

UNLOCKING YOUR VISUAL INTELLIGENCE

The first week of the program concludes with three exercises that provide step-by-step guidance in how to release the second key: the brain-expanding power of your visual IQ. All draw on innate picture smarts you use every day without suspecting their awesome possibilities. Day 5's exercise shows you how the shutter-like ability of the human eye to capture everything it "sees" in milliseconds can be developed to give you a "photographic memory." Day 6 helps you unlock the same genius for solving problems at a glance that made William Donaldson and Norman Schwarzkopf what they are today, while Day 7 showcases a dynamic new technique for acquiring skills, boosting performance, and transforming bad habits by just closing your eyes and daydreaming.

This may all seem like overclaiming, but it's not. Instead, this low opinion of our visual potential is the result of underestimating the true capacities of our visual intelligence.

Of all the body's senses, sight is the only one connected directly to the brain. Information from all the other senses has to travel through a long network of nerve cells before reaching the brain. But, your optical nerve runs straight back to your gray matter where it is wired directly to the occipital lobe, the seat of your visual IQ.

It's possible for a species to survive without language, the ability to reason, creativity, and intuition. But, vision is a basic for all living creatures higher than the worm. Without it they couldn't spot danger or locate succulent edibles from a distance. Nor could human beings design buildings, map DNA, surf the net, or navigate the Los Angeles freeways.

As a result, a high proportion of your gray matter is reserved for receiving, recording, and interpreting all that your eye sees, ensuring that all human beings are gifted with a generous share of picture smarts. Usually, only a few lucky individuals we hail as "artists" or business "geniuses" profit from unlocking the awesome possibilities of their visual IQ. But these three days offer a concentrated course in how increasing your visual intelligence can become instrumental in achieving success.

HOW YOU CAN BE AS SMART AS SHERLOCK HOLMES

It's easy to understand why visual intelligence might be valuable to an artist, architect, movie director, athlete, or professional race-car driver. It may not be as easy to understand how it could be important in your own life.

Our "shortsightedness" in this respect is due to an outdated conception of seeing as being about light carrying images to your retina—and nothing more. This led to the idea of visual intelligence as limited to interpreting images once they reach your eyes. Seeing, then, was considered limited to a passive act, in which light did all the work, and your picture smarts merely identified the images.

But now science tells us there is far more to seeing and far more to visual intelligence. Passive seeing is apparently a "default" setting—the minimum your image smarts are capable of, not the most. Apparently, we can take in ten times more visual information and make greater use of what we take in when we become proactive and make a conscious effort to see what's around us.

You can verify this for yourself right now. Close your eyes quickly at the end of this sentence and try to remember what everything looked like in the room around you (down to the tiniest detail) before you open them again.

Put this book down and compare what you recalled with what's actually before your eyes. What big things did you forget? That calendar on the wall? The bilious green of the lamp shade? What details did you miss? The way the carpet curls up in the corner? That large streak of dust on your monitor?

So how could you have overlooked all that? You had "seen" the room before you began reading, hadn't you? (You will probably also find you remember more of what you saw when you opened your eyes and made a conscious effort to see your environment.)

That's the difference between passive seeing and active seeing. When you focus your visual intelligence, you become more conscious of what you see, more aware of all the different things you are seeing, and more likely to recall what you have seen.

This is where making greater use of your visual IQ can play a role in your success. It can't be repeated too often, but the people on a fast track to fulfilling their dreams are the problem solvers of the world. Management is always on the "look" for employees with a facility for "spotting" solutions to difficulties and who can "see" more efficient ways to perform their jobs.

What does all this have to do with visual intelligence? When it comes to answering questions and solving problems, the more information you have, the more connections you can make, and the easier it becomes to find the answer. Becoming an active seer, rather than a passive one, gives you this extra edge. You consciously notice up to ten times more and hence have ten times more information for your brain to work with.

Sherlock Holmes's fabled genius as a detective was nothing more than active seeing: He consciously took in more of the subtle visual clues around him than did other people. But it isn't only fictional figures who have become successful through active seeing, as the following anecdote illustrates. (I challenge you to guess the real name of the celebrated figure involved, which appears at the end of the story.)

HOW VISUAL IQ HELPED ONE MAN SPOT A MILLION-DOLLAR OPPORTUNITY

Here's a success story everyone should recognize. It's about a man who had no special talent or ability; he wasn't an artist or an actor, and he certainly wasn't a genius in any traditional sense (his scholastic records prove that). Yet, when push came to shove, his visual IQ put him in the big time.

One day, as a young salesman for a milkshake-machine manufacturing company, this man noticed that one customer, a small neighborhood hamburger stand, had sent in an order for another six shake machines. Looking back, the young salesman realized it was the eighth time in three years he had seen such an order from the hamburger stand cross his desk. That made a total of forty-eight milkshake machines, and for the life of him the young salesman could not figure why a small neighborhood stand could need to make that many milkshakes at one time. So he decided to pay the stand a visit.

There he observed two brothers making hamburgers as fast as they could cook and serve them. To serve "fast food" this way to busy workers on short lunch breaks, they had simplified the standard operation, doing away with dishes, glasses, silverware, and all other food items, according to the menu, but hamburgers, french fries, soft drinks, and shakes. And they could hardly keep up with the orders.

The young salesman saw the brilliance, simplicity, and ingenuity of the idea. He conferred with the two brothers and soon reached an agreement to try to sell franchises copying their method of operation. The young salesman was named Ray Kroc, the two brothers, McDonald, and the outcome was the twentieth century's most successful fast-food franchise.

Kroc might not have noticed the pattern of orders coming in from the McDonald brothers. Or he might not have realized the simplicity and genius of their focus on serving a hamburger almost instantly to anyone who walked up. Merely by taking a little more notice of the information his eyes were bringing him, Ray Kroc developed an opportunity others had overlooked into a multimillion-dollar operation. It's a lesson we could all learn from.

EIGHT WAYS PICTURE SMARTS CAN MAKE YOU A VISUAL GENIUS

The capacities of your visual IQ extend far beyond active seeing. They include your ability to remember what you see, to spot subtle visual clues that escape others, even to harness your ability to daydream and mentally picture imaginary scenes as a method of overcoming destructive habits. In the three exercises that follow, the image smarts you unlock will help you

- Develop a photographic memory: take indelible mental snapshots of what you are looking at—at will: faces, documents, charts, physical locations

- Learn any job or skill you've seen someone demonstrate: golf strokes, knitting, operating the new document center

- Find anything you've put away or seen put away: old tax returns, lucky cuff links, that magazine clipping you stored two years ago, that one family photo your aunt wants to see

- Grasp and evaluate information in visual form: graphs, maps, charts, blueprints, tables

- Make answers to problems with a visual aspect "leap out" instantly: assembly lines, flow charts, productive use of space

- Spot critical opportunities in the world around you that other people miss: cost-cutting efficiencies, business prospects, construction jobs, athletic performance

- Mentally rehearse by visualizing: successful outcomes, practicing skills, public speeches

One particular portion of image smarts, imagery (Day 7), has even aided millions of people in firing motivation, managing emotions, overcoming addictions, and transforming dysfunctional behaviors into positive, healthy ones, freeing them to realize dreams they long thought out of reach.

FIVE PROVEN STRATEGIES FOR UNLOCKING YOUR VISUAL IQ

If, when you have completed the exercises for visual intelligence, you are interested in further expanding your picture smarts, I recommend the following mini-exercises. (They may also be helpful if you have to rush off before you can begin today's exercise and are anxious to commence boosting your visual intelligence at once. You can also practice these whereever you go.)

1. *Begin thinking in pictures rather than words.* Don't think the sentence, "I will do such a good job of researching this report, they will have to give me the promotion." Instead, picture yourself sitting at the computer, digging up all the figures on the web, and transferring them carefully to your report.

2. *Exercise your picture smarts.* Tour brightly colored floral displays at the local botanical gardens, drop in at an art exhibition, watch videos by a director noted for visual flair (John Ford, Ken Russell, Tim Burton), subscribe to *Life, The National Geographic,* or other publication famed for pictorial content.

3. *Light a candle.* This will help develop your picture smarts' ability to visualize scenes and images. Stare deeply into the heart of the flame for a count of twenty. Then shut your eyes. You will see the afterimage of the flame against your lids. Imagine you are seeing the actual flame. With your eyes still closed, use your "mind's eye" to visualize this flame growing larger and brighter. Picture this flame floating up free from the wick. Picture it floating right. Picture it floating left. (The afterimage should follow your imaginary flame.) Open your eyes and look at the actual candle flame for a moment. Then blow it out.

4. *Include all the senses, not just the visual, when exercising your picture smarts.* This will help make the scenes you visualize become even more vivid and detailed. Imagine whatever sounds, scents, tastes, and other sensations you would actually experience if what you are picturing were real.

5. *Practice regularly for maximum benefit.* As with any other muscle-development program, if you haven't been accustomed to exercising your picture smarts, they are likely to be rusty at first. But the more you use your visual intelligence the stronger it will become.

PUTTING THE POWER OF IMAGES TO WORK FOR YOU

The technique on the next page starts you on the path to super-sizing your picture smarts. You will learn how to develop your visual intelligence's ability to take a mental snapshot and turn it into the kind of photographic recall you have always dreamed of. The second exercise guides you in unlocking the kind of visual intelligence that made Sherlock Holmes such a wizard of detection, drawing on your innate ability to recognize and identify visual patterns. The final exercise coaches you in a unique form of "imagery," a facet of visual IQ scientifically proven to be a major tool for personal change and self-improvement.

EXERCISE: PHOTOGRAPHIC MEMORY

Prepare to develop an ability you thought you could never possess. You probably believed people with "photographic" memories were a small elite and that in order to remember in detail everything their eyes take in, someone had to be born with this special talent. But, those famed for remembering all that they see have the same measure of visual intelligence as everyone else. They have merely unlocked more of it than the average person.

Everyone has wished for the power of photographic recall. Today, you are going to begin to acquire that knack by drawing on your picture smarts a whole new way. You will actually learn to take an instantaneous "photograph" with your eye.

This process works in a way very similar to the way a camera shutter takes a color snapshot. It super-sizes your picture smarts by making use of newly discovered facts about how visual intelligence works, unlocking a hidden genius you already possess. Research indicates your innate visual IQ is so high it can snap a mental picture in fractions of a second if you ask it to and can retrieve that image, like a picture stored on a CD-ROM, years later.

A GOVERNOR'S AID ACCOMPLISHES THE IMPOSSIBLE

An obscure insect, inadvertently introduced from another country, had mushroomed overnight into an insect invasion that was threatening to devour one state's agricultural production. The governor appointed his agricultural aid, Ramone L., to research the issue thoroughly and prepare a "white paper" to be delivered at a major press conference just eighteen hours away.

Using his "pull" as a governor's aid, Ramone requisitioned everything available from the local and state university libraries and had it delivered to his desk within a few hours. Meanwhile, one of Ramone's assistants performed a crash-priority search of the internet, downloading hundreds of additional pages of facts, figures, charts, and graphs pertaining to the troublesome arthropod.

With fifteen hours to go, facing an "all-nighter," it would have been understandable for Ramone to feel intimidated, or even overwhelmed, by the daunting pile of pages that swamped his desk. But, as Ramone told me later, he looked upon this mass of reading material with equanimity, knowing there was ample time for him to review it all and dictate the paper the governor needed, well in advance of his deadline.

Why? What gave Ramone his marvelous poise and assurance in the face of a reading challenge that might well have deterred a librarian, William Buckley, or some other reading prodigy?

Ramone began to turn the pages quickly, literally photographing each key page mentally as it went by. At one of my workshops several years earlier, he had mastered the same photographic-memory technique described here. By now, he had developed his visual intelligence to the point where he knew he could take an indelible "picture" of anything—and everything—he found important.

Ramone was even able to complete the research and the paper in time to catch a two-hour nap and a change of clothes. He looked fresh and shaven standing at the governor's side during the press conference, as the governor read from the text Ramone had prepared.

WHY ANYONE CAN DEVELOP A PHOTOGRAPHIC MEMORY

When you blink, your eye opens and closes in about *one-half second.* When you "click" the shutter on a camera, on the other hand, it opens, closes, and takes its picture in only *thousandths of a second.* Yet, even in that fraction of time, the film captures a complete, full-color image of the world before it, and one strong enough to produce a crystal-clear photograph.

"Your brain has the same capacity," writes educational consultant Michael J. McCarthy, who specializes in accelerated learning. "Even receiving input for a fraction of a second, your brain is able to register many bits of information. You can use your eyes like the lens on a camera, taking a picture at a very fast shutter speed."

You can prove this for yourself and discover the astonishing ability of your picture smarts to "capture" visual information instantly. Shut your eyes, then open and close them quickly, and review all that you saw. However fast you were, your visual intelligence captured a recognizable portion of what was before your eyes—and in color.

What a truly amazing mechanism your brain is to take in all that information in a split second—just the way a camera does. The image is there, stored now in your memory. To develop this "photographic" capacity into a photographic memory, all you need to do is strengthen the connection between your conscious mind and your visual intelligence (where the images your eye captures are stored).

HOW YOUR EYE CAN TAKE PHOTOGRAPHS LIKE A CAMERA

The super brain power exercise you are about to learn is based on a radical reversal in scientific conceptions of how visual memory works. Previously, it was thought that the longer you stare at a picture, the more you will remember it. Both logically and intuitively, this conception would seem to make sense: The greater amount of time an image has to impress itself in your memory, the better you should be able to recall it.

But this is one instance where common sense is wrong. It turns out that, so far as seeing goes, less is more, and a great deal less translates into a whole lot more. Research into visual intelligence has revealed an astonishing fact. As McCarthy writes in *Mastering the Information Age*, "The faster we go, the more information we can absorb."

How can this be? Because of a simple principle: Objects are easier to remember when seen in context than they are when seen alone. Like words and musical notes, which gain significance as part of a melody or story, individual objects take significance as part of a picture. For example, you are watching a movie on television. As the camera begins to pan across a scene, you can fill in the gaps and tell what the remainder of the shot is going to show.

When you capture an image quickly with your eyes like a camera, your eyes are registering not just random objects, but objects in context. Looking at a picture, or a chart, or a page, each individual object is glimpsed within a larger context, enhancing comprehension and retention. Though the time spent looking at the image is brief, your picture smarts immediately grasps the objects, relates them to each other, and stores them in your visual memory banks.

The evidence even suggests that the longer you look at something, the less likely you are to recall all the details. How often have you walked into a friend's house, noticed a picture on the wall, and asked when your friend acquired it, only to be told it was there all along? Or, what about the proverbial husband who fails to notice his spouse's new hairstyle?

You have experienced this if you have ever found yourself reading so slowly that when you finally reach the end of the sentence or paragraph, you discover you had forgotten how it started and what it was about. Reading word by word like this causes you to lose the significance of the whole, so that you have to backtrack and look at the material again. Reading quickly, rather than being a hindrance, allows your visual intelligence to grasp the essential content, the whole picture. The individual parts then add to your understanding of the whole.

The same is true when you are watching a motion picture. If you stopped the film long enough to see each individual frame, you would see only a series of still photographs, each minutely different from the rest. But when it is run at full speed, actors walk, talk, kiss, and drive cars in what appears to be continuous motion. The individual frames create meaning for your eye only because it is taking them in so quickly that they become a continuous, coherent whole, their significance created entirely by their relationship and context.

While you consciously register only a few objects, subconsciously your visual intelligence is picking up far more. That's why you can retain images better when you quickly open and close your eyes like a camera shutter than by staring at them trying to soak up every detail.

FOUR WAYS THIS EXERCISE SUPER-SIZES YOUR SUCCESS FACTOR

The pluses of a photographic memory can't be oversold. Being able to pull facts, figures, faces, details of charts, plans, memos, and whether there were two exits large enough for trucks in that storage facility the school board is considering purchasing ensures you an inside track in almost any kind of situation. Using this exercise to boost your ability to remember what you see increases your likelihood of success in whatever endeavor you choose. Once you have acquired experience in practicing this technique, you will be able to mentally photograph and recall

- All that you see: faces, places, events, that new organizational chart the CEO presented, the golf grip your partner showed you this morning

- Where you and others put or stored anything: that videotaped sales presentation, lost keys, old files, last year's holiday decorations

- The printed page: memos, reports, abstracts, textbooks, journals, books, and other documents

- Physical locations: construction sites, plant interiors and equipment, warehouses

VISUAL INTELLIGENCE BUILDER: PHOTOGRAPHIC MEMORY

When I say that you are going to learn to capture a mental photograph of any scene, object, or page the same way you do with a camera, I mean exactly that. As with film and camera, it's a two-stage process. First you will learn how to use your eyes like a shutter to take the picture with your eyes. Then you will learn how to develop it mentally.

Before you begin, please take the time to read all the instructions through and be certain you understand them. You will benefit more from this exercise if you don't have to interrupt yourself by referring back to the book while practicing it.

PART I. TAKING YOUR PICTURE

1. Sit down at a table and place a closed book or magazine that is full of color photographs and illustrations on the table before you.

2. Close your eyes, and by touch alone, open to any page at random.

3. With your eyes shut, tilt your head down at the page you have opened. Then blink your eyes open and shut three times rapidly, ending with them shut, as if your eye were the high-speed shutter of a camera taking a picture of the page.

PART II. DEVELOPING YOUR PICTURE

4. With your eyes still closed from the end of your third blink, the afterimage of the page you looked at should show brightly against your lids. Strengthen it by trying to recall first the most memorable object. It may have been in the center, it may have been something vividly colored. Whatever it is, that object will be easiest to see. Try to picture it as realistically as possible, and it will probably quickly become clear in your mind's eye.

5. Still with your lids tightly shut, ask yourself what are the next most memorable objects? They will probably begin to take shape as you ask. Again, try to "see" them in full color and detail in the exact positions they occupied around your most memorable object. The images may come a little more slowly. But, if you are patient, it should take less than two minutes to see them all clearly.

6. Now, picture the next most memorable objects. It may take you a little longer, but here's a tip: If you have difficulty, try to fill in the blank spots between the objects you have already visualized. You may find it easier to recall what the objects were this way.

7. Finally, do your best to recall and see any other details. Again, to help jog your visual memory, try to picture what was filling up the spaces between the objects you already remember.

For best results, repeat this exercise several times immediately, turning to a different page each time. The result should be detailed mental photographs of illustrations you caught only three microsecond glimpses of. That should be sufficient proof you can develop photographic memory of your own.

As you become more practiced in the photographic-memory technique, you will find yourself taking in larger and larger gulps of visual data at one time. Harnessing using your parallel conscious and subconscious visual systems in tandem, like this, will eventually enable you to take in whole pages of information at a glance.

THE POWER TECHNIQUE YOU'LL LEARN TOMORROW

The next visual intelligence builder, "power seeing," will empower you to quickly assimilate information and solve problems presented in visual form: graphs, maps, charts, plans, sports, assembly lines, storage.

DAY 6 ———————————————————————————————————
EXERCISE: POWER SEEING

Today you will learn a visual strategy that will place you in a league with the world's greatest troubleshooters. You may wonder how someone like Lee Iacocca and other celebrated "turnaround" geniuses are able to accomplish their headline-generating successes. They walk into a position as CEO of an ailing multinational, in an unfamiliar line of business, and know almost miraculously which divisions and personnel to keep and which to trim in order to restore fiscal health without dealing the company a mortal blow.

It's the same talent, though it might not seem so at first, that allows an experienced foreperson to look at a set of blueprints for a home and instantly "see" and solve construction problems the architect overlooked. It's what make it possible for plumbers, carpenters, electricians, and handypersons to look at their work and know what needs to be done next, or that allows financial wizards and accountants to absorb graphs, charts, and tables at a glance, all without ever putting their thoughts into words.

It's the aspect of visual intelligence at play when you look at a half-finished brick fence and know where the black and white bricks should go to complete it in the same zigzag pattern the builders began. Or that allows you to look at a chart, and in a series of confusing ups and downs, discern a slow tendency downward. Or to look at a computer screen and recognize without reading any of the instructions which portions are data fields you will need to fill in.

Scientists have labeled this ability "pattern recognition." This big-sounding phrase is nothing more than your visual IQ's ability to mentally put together and picture a whole image from just a few of its parts. The following exercise provides step-by-step guidance in super-sizing your brain power through an advanced form of pattern recognition I call "power seeing."

THE NATURAL POWER THAT MAKES YOU A VISUAL GENIUS

"Power seeing" is a natural, effective technique for gaining visual knowledge and finding answers to visual problems quickly and effectively. It has helped many people to success and is based on our picture smart's wonderful ability to mentally assemble a whole picture from incomplete parts. In fact, this portion of your hidden genius is designed to automatically find meaning and pattern in as few visual clues as possible and to fill in or transpose elements to reach closure.

Pattern recognition is another of those capacities hardwired in your brain and inherited from when our ancestors roved the African grasslands. They had to be able to tell friend from enemy and predatory carnivores from harmless herd animals. From just a few dark splotches against a yellow background they had to put together the visual cues that spelled the difference between a leopard and an antelope—in a hurry, and from far away—before the intruder drew near enough to do damage if it was a danger.

Your visual intelligence automatically

- Scans for and recognizes patterns

- Searches those patterns for larger meaning that could fit them within a picture

- Seeks visual closure by generating a whole image from its available portions

Here's how it works. When new visual data—images or portions of images—come in through the senses your visual intelligence they immediately scour through millions of previously stored images searching for matches. They convert the raw sensory input about color, shape, relationship of size and distance, and so on into images that were meaningful in the context of your experience. Your image smarts seem to inquire, "Is anything familiar here? Is there a pattern I can recognize?"

When you are asked to guess something like the next number in the sequence 565656565, you probably have no difficulty in guessing "6." That's because the mind is concerned with meanings. It doesn't passively absorb one individual fact or image or word. Instead, it hunts for a pattern or context within which they have a larger significance. We remember a baseball statistic, or the love scene in a movie, or a memorable paragraph in a book, not because of the numbers themselves, or another picture of two people kissing, or the individual words, but because of the larger meaning that they convey to us within that context.

You can demonstrate for yourself just how this process works by reading the following paragraph. Don't struggle to puzzle it out and read word by word. Scan through it quickly, and you will discover the way your visual intelligence automatically fills in the missing letters and recognizes the whole word.

> At th sme tm yr vsul intlgnc is rcvng dta frm yr eys it is als intrptng tht dta. Ths mns yu dn't ned to se al th prts to rcognz th whl. In mny cses, yu rcognz pple an objcs frm thr gnrl ftrs an otlns, lng bfor yu ar clos enug to mke ut th dtals.

If you are like most people, your image smarts filled in the missing vowels without much effort. Visual intelligence searched for pattern, completed the meaning, and your understanding of the individual words and the paragraph as a whole was as clear as if every letter had been there in the first place.

VISUAL INTELLIGENCE BUILDER: POWER SEEING

The following three-part power-seeing technique starts you toward a level of pattern recognition usually associated only with the big winners in life. Each of the three parts will give you conscious practice in unlocking your brain's natural ability to take fragmentary clues, identify meaning, and reach closure by assembling them into the pattern they create.

PART I

This portion of the exercise is a "warm-up" for your visual intelligence. Think of yourself as doing mental "stretches" to limber and strengthen your visual intelligence before you start more difficult exercises and to get you accustomed to consciously using its pattern-recognition capacities. As you read through the household phrases below, your visual intelligence should automatically comprehend the whole and supply the missing words. Fill in all the blanks you can with a pen or pencil.

Mary _____ a little _____, it's _____ was white as _____.

Ships that _____ in the _____.

A _____ saved is a _____ earned.

Something is _____ in the state of _____.

The early _____ gets the _____.

London _____ is _____ down.

Early to _____ early to _____, keeps a _____ healthy, _____ and _____.

It's not likely you had very much trouble with any of them. Yet we rarely think of pattern recognition as a talent we can rely on when we need it.

PART II

Now that you know your image smarts will automatically detect patterns in numbers, you can further build your confidence in its powers. Give it some exercise in consciously detecting visual patterns. Seven shapes in the following illustration are similar. Chances are, your visual IQ is so acute you will identify them at first glance.

Even though they are different sizes, your image smarts had no difficulty picking out the seven circles as sharing a similar shape. As simple as this exercise may have seemed, it firmly establishes your visual intelligence's amazing capacity to instantly discern and identify patterns.

Part III

Try this more advanced exercise. It challenges your visual intelligence to identify more subtle patterns. It may even require the simultaneous interplay of other intelligences as well. Each of the following three sequences of numbers has a pattern. Your visual intelligence will probably make quick work of finding and recognizing that pattern. Identify the pattern in the blank that follows each line.

20, 18, 16, 14, 12, 10, 8, 6, 4, 2, _____.

2, 4, 16, 256, 65, 536, 4, 294, 967, 296, _____.

2, 4, 8, 16, 32, 64, 128, _____.

It's important to emphasize that in answering the questions asked in the preceding three sections, you weren't merely recognizing visual patterns, you were also solving problems. Here, you have an excellent illustration of your own mind's awe-inspiring potentials for visual problem solving.

PART IV

Now that you have learned something of your visual IQ's power for detecting patterns and solving visual problems by filling in the blanks, it's time to consciously start applying it to real-life situations. Once you master this kind of "power seeing," you will find yourself taking light-year-long steps forward in the depth and complexity of the problems you can solve.

1. *Throughout your day, notice the visual patterns around you.* You will find them in columns of expense and income reports, in accident statistics, in bond market fluctuations, in weather averages. You will also find that if you see an interrupted or broken pattern, your seeing smarts will fill in the rest.

2. *Focus in on the buildings, fences, parking lots, and other physical constructions.* Look for the patterns (they are there, you just may not have noticed them). Chain-link fences may seem to have diamond patterns, or big Xs. Buildings may have decorative brick or tile work that make zigzag, turreted, checkerboard, or other patterns. Cars in a supermarket parking lot could be parked at random throughout the lot, or all parked in long rows in two or three lines.

3. *Focus in on the designs on the clothing people wear.* Look for the patterns and you will find such a profusion, you may be overwhelmed: polka dot, paisley prints, stripes, checks, complementary colors, deliberately clashing colors. You will even notice patterns in styles: profusions of single-breasted suits, miniskirts, stirrup pants, oxfords, and on and on.

4. *Focus in on the way people act.* Look for patterns in similarities and in differences. A friend may always cross himself when something good happens; a coworker may close her office door after the Friday marketing meeting every week; your lover may brighten up every time you make plans for an evening at the movies—and from these you may glean clues to his or her personality and motives.

5. *Focus in on a real-life problem you have been grappling with that has a visual element.* For example, at the office you might observe the pattern that your personal assistant is losing up to an hour a day because she has to jump up every few minutes and walk across the room to use the copier. Or you may, as I did, have a small three-by-four-foot nook into which you must fit fifty-five boxes of memorabilia with about five different kinds of shapes that your mother has just had shipped to your front door. Or you may have a problem on a production line where things are going smoothly for the person who snaps the arms and legs on the dolls, but there is a bottleneck where the person is painting the detailing on a toy.

6. *Focus in on the pattern to find a solution.* In fact, the solution is often implicit in your formulation of the problem, and that will be enough for your visual intelligence to leap instantly to a viable solution. In the example of your secretary losing an hour or more a day crossing the room to the copy machine, it makes sense to save her effort and the company time by relocating the copier near her desk, or vice-versa. When I was stuck with all those cartons and a small storage space, I looked for patterns in the kinds of boxes and found five different sizes; and I knew that I could easily figure out the best arrangement by placing one of each sized box on the floor of the nook and shifting them around until they fitted snugly, then stacking all the same-size boxes on top of each other up to the ceiling. As for the assembly line, clearly it was easier and faster to snap the arms, legs, and head on than to paint the details when the dolls were assembled, so you might have added a second person to the painting station, to speed things up.

The more time you invest in looking for, and troubleshooting with, patterns such as this, the greater your facility for power seeing will become. More important, you will find your visual intelligence filling in any gaps, pinpointing the larger context or meaning, and solving any problems they present.

HOW POWER SEEING HELPED ONE PERSON WIN A PROMOTION

Loring was Southeast Asia purchasing agent for FedRate (not real name), a large U.S. chain of discount department stores. Socially conscious, the chain insisted he beware of doing business with suppliers that ran "sweatshop" type operations, exploiting or abusing employees. One of FedRate's best Southeast Asia suppliers had been targeted by labor activists as such a company. But inspection of the company's factories two years earlier by top FedRate officials had found an exemplary operation, everything bright and clean, every employee well-dressed and cheerful. When additional charges was aimed at the company, it prompted corporate officials to send Loring, as their man on the spot, to conduct a follow-up examination.

Loring was a master of pattern recognition. He had taught me a good deal about its importance. He noted the spotless white walls and the spotless white tables the employees worked at and that the employees were dressed in fresh, clean jeans and shirts. But he also observed one or two other things that his visual IQ added up a very different pattern.

The whitewash on the walls, floors, and desk tops was still wet around the edges. The legs and undersides of the desks were grubby and caked with filth. The employees' clothing may made it look as if the people were sufficiently well paid. But their teeth, hair, nails, and hands were less clean and suggested they actually lived without water or electricity.

These and other clues caused Loring to alert FedRate to a possible pattern in which the whitewashed walls and neat attire were merely camouflage the company trotted out to deceive its U.S. clients. When FedRate paid private detectives to initiate a more extensive investigation, Loring's suppositions were confirmed. Impressed with his observational genius, Loring was brought into the home office and made vice president in charge of European purchasing.

You've probably gotten the idea by now, but I do also want to mention Bill, a banker friend in Baton Rouge, Louisiana. One day while double-checking a long list of deposits and withdrawals on his computer at work, a subtle pattern leaped out at him. Payouts over one hundred dollars by one new cashier always ended in $25. That all the people who came to his window for large withdrawals would want cash ending in these two figures seemed unlikely. After a short investigation, Bill found the cashier routinely adding $25 to any cash withdrawal over one hundred dollars and pocketing the difference himself, foolishly thinking the amount was so small no one would notice.

THE POWER TECHNIQUE YOU'LL LEARN TOMORROW

The last day of visual intelligence will familiarize you with a newly discovered application of "visualization." Here you have heard about the astonishing powers of visualization and how they have helped carry people to success in all walks of life. You may even make use of them yourself. But tomorrow you are going to encounter a brand-new wrinkle, guaranteed to elevate your overall brain power.

EXERCISE: POWER IMAGERY

How would you like to know one simple, three-minute exercise that you can use to develop and perfect any skill, end undesirable habits, and generate positive behaviors—plus help you build the motivation to reach new heights? A unique, super brain power version of a proven technique that top figures in business, athletics, the professions, arts, and self-development—people such as Zig Ziglar, Mary Kay Ash, Rick Pitino, Kareem Abdul Jabar, Kathy Rigby, Tony Robbins, and Marianne Williamson—hail as the key to their success? Today's exercise is all that and more.

This technique will build on your innate ability to "see" things in your imagination. If you can picture a tropical isle, or the perfect wedding dress, or what it would be like to see your name on the door to the CEO's office, then you will have no difficulty unlocking your hidden visual genius with power imagery.

WHAT THE POWER OF THE MIND'S EYE CAN DO FOR YOU

You have probably read about "imagery," also known as "visualization" or "the mind's eye." It is an aspect of picture smarts everyone shares. It's another of those traits that not only appear to distinguish us from the other animals, but is responsible for carrying humankind a significant portion of the distance from the cave to the digital age. (Without some cave person's ability to envision it first, no one would ever have thought to carry fire from a lightning-struck tree back to the cave, where it could keep everyone warm and safe at night.)

Imagery, for all its scientific-sounding name, is nothing more or less than your capacity to "picture" things visually in your imagination. It could be sudden recall of a scene from childhood so complete you can see literally every detail. It could be a vivid daydream of sitting before that mountain cabin you have always yearned to own, painting the landscapes you have always yearned to create. It could be a momentary vision within the mind's eye of how that pile of student papers you have to grade will look when you are finished and can place them in your "out" box.

The ability to visualize objects and scenes in your mind's eye might seem trivial, or something that's only of use to those in the creative professions. But it turns out to produce extraordinary physical and mental results.

Imagining a situation stirs the same emotions as does the actual situation. Picture your most humiliating childhood experience. For most people this is enough to cause them to reexperience the cringing shame they felt at the time. Next, try to visualize the funniest thing you ever saw, and likely even a dim image is enough to bring at least a smile back to your face. Finally, picture your most successful moment, graduating from college, the first time your boss praised you publicly, or the soccer championship where you made the winning goal. Again, you will probably feel something of the actual triumphant emotions you experienced then.

Imagery's ability to stir emotions and physical reactions has many benefits. You can understand why sales pros and gold-medal athletes would embrace any technique that empowered them to summon enthusiasm when they are down, generate calm when they are upset, and build courage in the face of difficulty. And all this is only the beginning.

Imagining a movement stimulates the same nerve pathways as does actually making the movement. Science has discovered another benefit to imagery. Just as picturing a scene can stimulate your emotions, so picturing yourself performing an act activates the same muscles, nerves, and brain cells as does performing the act. In short, you can learn or improve a skill by visualizing yourself practicing, just as you can by actually practicing it.

Performance consultant James Manketlow, whose "Mind Tools" website is a massive resource for those interested in self-transformation, explains, "Much of the process of learning and improving sporting reflexes and skills is the laying down, modification, and strengthening of nerve pathways in our body and brains. These pathways can be effectively trained by the use of mental techniques such as imagery and simulation." This finding, James Manketlow notes, has been applied successfully by sports figures, business professionals, and millions of other people to acquiring new abilities and boosting performance.

NINE WAYS IMAGERY CAN HELP YOU TOWARD SUCCESS

The applications of imagery have proved nearly endless and extend into nearly every area of life.

In the areas of productivity and performance it has been used to:

1. *Learn new skills.* Carla spent the evenings mentally practicing the moves at her new station as manager at a fast-food restaurant.

2. *Enhance performance.* Wilber pictured his backstroke in ultra-slow motion, analyzing each step for faults he could remedy and strengths he could identify.

3. *Rehearse mentally.* LuAnne reduced her anxiety at having to make a speech by rehearsing it mentally until she knew she was letter-perfect.

4. *Prepare for difficulty.* Mort pictured various objections prospective clients might make to his sales presentation, so he was able to overcome them on the spot.

5. *Fire motivation.* Sean came in first in the contest his office was running by keeping his enthusiasm high through envisioning every detail of the tropical vacation he would win if he sold the most real estate.

In the area of personal change and improvement, imagery has been proven effective at:

1. *Managing emotions.* Ilene pictured herself as remaining calm and collected in the face of provocations to help manage her anger.

2. *Ending addictions.* Zach visualized himself walking past his liquor bottles and working off his upsets in his garden, rather than take a drink, to help end his alcoholism.

3. *Controlling destructive behaviors.* Emanuel envisioned eating delicious, but *healthful* meals to reduce his consumption of sugar and fats.

4. *Engendering positive habits.* Ramone, who was very passive, pictured himself being more assertive in various office scenarios.

POWER IMAGERY: ONE STEP TO SELF-TRANSFORMATION

This advanced visual IQ technique for fostering healthful behaviors and ending undesirable habits is based on two recent scientific findings. The first is that before we do anything, the brain must form a mental picture of us performing the act. (This process is almost entirely unconscious, such as when we walk across a room and open a door, or decide to drive to the mall.)

The second finding is that bad habits are so hard to change—and good ones are so difficult to implant—because by the time we become adults, most situations automatically trigger a picture of how we typically react to them. Being bullied, for instance, might produce an image of you retreating into passivity, a stressful situation an image of pouring a drink, an intimidating assignment of procrastinating by goofing off. Then we proceed to act in accordance with the picture.

Current research suggests you can't change these behaviors, unless you first change the unconscious picture the situation triggers. Otherwise, most people continue to act in conformity with that image, despite willpower, motivational seminars, psychotherapy, assertiveness, recovery groups, anger management classes, and other behavior-modification systems. But with power imagery, the psychological mechanism that has been causing your problem is turned in its tracks and put to work in your behalf. You can use power imagery as a kind of mental jujitsu to automatically transform the image of your undesirable responses into those of positive, desirable behaviors, instead.

You can use power imagery to

- Stop bad habits and self-defeating behaviors
- Overcome fears and doubts
- Confidently face intimidating situations
- Establish healthful, desirable habits and thoughts

VISUAL INTELLIGENCE BUILDER: POWER IMAGERY

Here's how you can use power imagery to transform unwanted character traits and develop the confidence to conquer any challenge:

1. *Form a clear detailed mental "photograph" of the behavior you want to change.* Even see the border around the photograph. In the examples mentioned earlier in this chapter, you would picture yourself sitting silent and passive while being unfairly bullied by a coworker, or opening a Scotch bottle and taking a drink after receiving stressful news.

2. *Form a similar picture of what you will be like when this improvement is made.* See yourself feeling satisfied after having stood up for yourself and politely but firmly having spoken your mind to a bully; or form a detailed image of the emotional glow you will have after meditating or taking a long walk to work off stress and anger; or create a mental snapshot of you leaning back in your chair with a smile of satisfaction, that intimidating assignment completed and already out of your hands.

3. *Make your mind blank for a moment, then visualize your photograph of the behavior you want to change,* with the photo of the way you want things to be smaller and darker in the lower right-hand corner.

4. *Visualize the smaller image suddenly growing in brightness and dimension* and bursting through the photograph of the behavior you want to alter in a flash. And at the same time, say "Change!" to yourself as energetically as possible. (Linking an image to a word charged with emotional energy like this impresses the image more deeply in your visual intelligence.)

5. *Let yourself bask in this bright, exciting picture of things the way you desire them to be.*

6. *Open your eyes for a moment, to interrupt the imagery state.*

7. *Repeat steps #3 to #5 between four and five times*, as quickly and as rapidly as possible.

In the future, you can face similar situations with assurance. As soon as your unconscious triggers a picture of you responding in the old, unhealthy way, the image of its healthy opposite should spontaneously "burn" through and replace it in your mind's eye. If it doesn't, simply say "change" and trigger the process yourself. "For best results," writes Anthony Robbins, "the key is repetition and rapidity." Eventually, it's the image of the desirable behavior that will be set off automatically, and the image of the bad habit will no longer be triggered at all.

How Crandall Conquered His Fear of Flying With Power Imagery

Crandall was a nature photographer who freelanced for several publications in the big city where he lived. Though he made good money, his lifelong dream was to hit the big time and become a staff photographer for *The National Geographic*. Crandall also had a lifelong fear, and that was flying. He was petrified and simply couldn't get on a plane. Although he had covered most of the United States in the course of his work, Crandall had always driven there.

He came to me in an emotional tailspin one day because his dream of working for *National Geographic* was on the verge of coming true, but it had come into collision with his phobia about flying. The magazine had at last offered Crandall a position as a roving photographer covering India and Asia, an assignment that would involve almost constant air travel.

I asked Crandall to describe the first image that came to his mind when he thought about flying. "I'm clutching the arm rests and screaming as the plane plunges down toward the ground about to crash!" he replied without hesitation.

I explained how power imagery worked and suggested Crandall book a flight to the *Geographic*'s home office for the next week. Until then, I asked him to work on overcoming his fear of flying with the power imagery exercise. The replacement picture was to be himself leaving the plane with a smile for the attendants at the end of a relaxing flight. Since Crandall's time was short, I recommended that for best results he pause three times every day until his departure and perform the exercise.

I didn't hear from Crandall for two years, when we met by chance at a movie screening. He looked fit and tan. When I asked him about his fear of flying, Crandall looked blank for a moment and then laughed. "I've flown so much the last couple of years, I'd almost forgotten I ever had a problem. That thing you taught me helped turn the trick. I didn't lose my fear immediately, of course. But it began to lessen enough right away that I could get on a plane. In fact, I had to keep it up before and during every flight for almost a year. But then one day I was so caught up in planning for an emergency shoot in Afghanistan that I found I was on the plane and halfway through the flight before I realized I hadn't even once thought about the plane crashing or experienced a moment of fear."

THE POWER TECHNIQUE YOU WILL LEARN TOMORROW

Prepare for four days that will give you detailed instruction in brain-friendly techniques that empower you to think as clearly and logically as a W. Clement Stone, Suze Orman, or Ken Radziwanowski.

DAYS 8–11

The Third Key—

UNLOCKING YOUR LOGICAL GENIUS

WHAT'S YOUR LOGICAL IQ?

This self-assessment test allows you to gauge the current extent of your logical intelligence. It's not a scientifically rigorous quiz, and scoring low doesn't mean you are some kind of dumbbell, deficient in thinking smarts. The four simple exercises that comprise the logical IQ part of this program will show you ways of doubling your thinking smarts, no matter who you are or how you perform on the following test.

Check the box beside any description that feels as if it applies to you. Do you typically

- ❐ Quickly add, multiply, subtract, and divide even large numbers in your head?

- ☑ Easily spot logical flaws in advertisements, political arguments, people's explanations?

- ❐ Constantly inquire into the how and why of things in science, events, other people's behavior, business, the natural world?

- ❐ Open the page to the stock-market reports or the science section every morning?

- ❐ Enjoy the challenge of tackling—and successfully solving— problems that baffle others?

- ❐ Relax during leisure time with computer strategy and role-playing games or working on books of brain-teasers?

- ❐ Do better in math and science classes than in English or history?

☐ Like to set up little "what-if" experiments (for example: "What if I double the amount of water I give to my rosebush each week?" Or, "What if I change my technique with the next prospect I call on and see how they react?")?

☑ Find a way to make things work or "jury-rig" a temporary solution, often from the most unlikely elements?

☐ Believe everything has a logical, rational explanation that can be found if you try hard enough or long enough?

☑ Enjoy excursions to planetariums, aquariums, museums, and other sites of education and edification?

☑ Feel more "comfortable" with things when they have been examined, quantified, and explained in detail?

☐ Subscribe to *Discover, Archeology, Forbes, Nation,* or other mentally stimulating publications?

☐ Carry a calculator in your briefcase, purse, or coat pocket?

☐ Like to amuse yourself and friends with logical paradoxes, rather than with jokes or puns?

☐ Recall as a child asking for chemistry sets and telescopes as presents on your birthday?

☐ Write clear, sufficiently detailed directions for reaching any a destination or performing the most complex task?

Scoring: Add up the number of boxes you checked.

If your score was between 1 and 4, this section of the super brain power program is what you need to resuscitate a logical IQ you have allowed to let become nearly moribund. Though you may feel you are a hopeless candidate for acquiring thinking smarts, the brain-friendly exercises that you are about to begin will soon have them vital and thriving again.

If your score was between 5 and 9, you break even with the day's challenges, but you aren't moving ahead in life. Problems often seem insurmountable, you have been victimized more often than you would care to admit, and your mathematical skills are nothing you are proud of. However, when the next four days are done, the logical intelligence portion of this book will have provided all the tools you need to reason your way through whatever difficulties you encounter in the course of your personal or professional rounds.

If your score was between 10 and 14, you are probably ahead of the pack at work, are either already a manager or have been slated as managerial material, have a well-deserved reputation for thinking smarts among your friends, find solutions to most difficulties, and aren't easily flummoxed by math. But with only a bit more effort, you could go straight to the heights of logical intelligence.

If your score was between 15 and 17, your logical IQ is so near the top there is little or no room for improvement. You could be a CEO or a scientist or a banker or even a professor of logic. These four days of exercises can't challenge your particular brand of thinking smarts, but being the logical type, you probably won't be able to rest until you have tested your wits against each one and proved it for yourself.

UNLOCKING YOUR LOGICAL INTELLIGENCE

It makes no difference how poorly you scored on the What's Your Logical IQ? quiz (page 105). Nor does it make any difference how minuscule is your estimation of your own thinking smarts. Your logical intelligence may be stiff from disuse but, like your legs after a week in bed with the flu, give it a bit of a workout and you will witness an astonishing advance in your ability to reason things through and solve even seemingly insoluble problems.

The words "logic" and "reason" intimidate most people. They conjure an image of the most rigorous kind of university examination. People tend to think "being logical" is a quality you are either born with or without. They suffer from the misconception that only geniuses such as Albert Einstein or Warren Bennis or Rosabeth Moss Kanter or Bill Gates are proficient at logical thinking.

But the fact is, logical thinking is as natural for us as breathing, walking, seeing, eating, and feeling. They are all hardwired in the brain, and so is our capacity for logical thinking. In fact, we all have millions of logic circuits: A whole section of the brain, the cerebral cortex, is given over to them.

We are reasoning all the time. The process is just so natural we never notice it. That's why we so often feel we aren't very logical. Unless our attention is directed toward it, we seldom become conscious of all the times during the day when we use logic as naturally as we open a door.

You're applying logic to solve problems any time you decide it's a better idea to do one thing rather than another. When you decide to keep the stapler in your top desk drawer, rather than the bottom, because you use it so often. When you decide to end your relationship with Bob because, after two years of dating, he still isn't interested in commitment. When you decide to compromise with your brother over how to portion your late mother's jewelry, to avoid an argument that would cause only hurt and contention. When you decide to place the potatoes on the grill first, because they take longer to cook than the steaks.

The four techniques that inaugurate the second week of the super brain power program show you how you can unlock this portion of your hidden genius to produce answers and arrive at choices you can be confident are intelligent, informed, and error free.

IT JUST MAKES SENSE: YOUR LOGICAL INTELLIGENCE AT WORK

Logical thinking, also called reasoning, is nothing more than deciding whether or not things "make sense" or "add up." How often have you used those phrases and said something to yourself like, "the instructions for this blender don't make sense" or "the new manager's explanation for why we aren't getting a bonus this year doesn't add up?" Every time you have, it was your logical intelligence in action.

That's all logical thinking is: putting two and two together to make four. And you are putting two and two together to make four all the time. If you can do that, you can learn to reason as accurately as a Nobel laureate.

In a way, logic is just another name for applied commonsense, and you were born with a fair share of that (whether you act on it or not). Stripped of all the academic decoration, logic is nothing more than deciding whether or not the facts support what someone says, or whether two facts fit together in the way someone claims.

You have all the abilities you need to send your logical IQ to the heights if you can do these two simple things:

1. *Tell if the evidence does or does* not *uphold an idea.* For example, "I think Tom is right. Three wrecks in two years means Lariat is an alcoholic." Or, "Martha has to be wrong about freezing ruining butter. I remember Mom froze it all the time and there was nothing wrong with the butter when we used it."

2. *Tell if two items do or do not add up to justify a conclusion.* "Yes, I think you are right. Sleeping with the window open all night during a raging snowstorm probably has something to do with my sniffles." Or, "I don't think eating peanut butter before going to the beach made your sunburn worse."

This is the logical equivalent of adding two plus two. It may seem simple, but so are addition and subtraction when you learn them in primary school. And, like them, it opens up a new world of possibilities once you begin to realize its applications.

How Bill Lear Put "One" Plus "One" Together to Make Millions

In fact, using your logical intelligence is even easier than "two plus two makes four." If you can add one plus one to make two, you can become an overnight success, as the following story shows.

In the 1920s, Bill Lear, a young engineering graduate took a job with Galvin, a division of Motorola, which manufactured radio chassis. It was an era when many a young man and woman was getting rich by thinking of simple devices to lighten the burdens of work or to add a creature comfort to people's lives.

Lear was out driving his model T one day, when his thoughts turned to a favorite radio program he was missing. He realized immediately that other people must feel the same way. Soon he was working out the details of what became the first successful automobile radio.

Lear's invention made him wealthy enough to indulge several longtime passions. One was flying his own airplane. In the course of various flights across country, Lear discovered why flying was typically restricted to daytime and why aerial navigation them was considered so chancy.

In those days, the only way pilots had to tell where they were going was to keep an eye out for familiar landmarks below: rivers, mountains, cities. If the craft encountered clouds or fog, the pilot either had to land immediately or risk becoming lost and crashing.

Lear immediately began sketching out a prototype of his "Learoscope," which instituted the modern age of air flight and is still, in amplified form, the basis of all aircraft navigation today. Lear's invention allowed each airport to broadcast an identifiable, individual radio signal, so pilots stay on course simply by noting which fields they were passing—and could home in on the correct landing field—even at night and in dense fog.

When the U.S. military pioneered the jet plane during the Korean War and the big airlines began to adopt them for passenger travel, Lear yearned for a small private jet of his own. Since nothing like that was being produced, Lear decided to form his own company and build them himself. The Learjet, too, became a huge commercial success.

In each case, Bill Lear made a fortune, simply by adding one plus one and getting two. People like to drive cars and listen to radio, hence the car radio. Airplane pilots needed an accurate way of navigating, radio signals could be picked up from miles away, hence using radio signals to guide pilots. People were getting interested in jets, no one was making small jets for private pilots, hence making them. Making a million dollars can be just that easy.

THINKING SMARTS: THE KEY TO PERSONAL AND PROFESSIONAL SUCCESS

The ability to solve problems through logical thinking is fundamental to professional success. It's what scholastic evaluation tests are based on. It's the first quality that employers look for in potential employees.

Though it's less apparent, a facility for thinking smarts is fundamental to success in personal life as well. The ability to resolve critical problems may be even more vital in the "school of hard knocks" than in the halls of academe: from what career to pursue (or whether to change one), to whom to marry (or not marry), to how to raise the money to meet that sudden bill for back taxes, to whether an elderly parent would be better off in her own home or in a nursing home.

Yet, logical thinking is never taught in school, beyond the rudiments of "inductive" and "deductive" reasoning in a few simple axioms such as, "If A = B and B = C, then A = C." Since this is pretty abstract stuff for grade schoolers and even middle schoolers, it goes over our heads. We "don't get it," feel like dunces, and decide logic isn't for us or we are too dense to be good at it.

The problem isn't that we were somehow shorted at birth when it comes to logical IQ. The problem lies with the way the educational system goes about introducing us to the subject, which leaves us with such a low opinion of our logical intelligence.

What too often holds us back from success, or from solving a major problem, isn't lack of logical intelligence, but lack of *confidence* in our logical intelligence. You've probably heard the expression that someone's "confidence in their abilities was misplaced," meaning they mistakenly believed they could do something only to fall flat on their face. If your appraisal of your thinking smarts finds them wanting, you are in precisely the opposite situation. It's your *lack* of confidence in your abilities that's misplaced; you are in the position of someone who's afraid he will fall flat on his face, someone who already has the capacity to "ace" the whole thing with ample brain power left over.

FIVE WAYS YOUR LOGICAL IQ MAKES YOU A GENIUS

Picture yourself telling a prospective employer *not* to give you any job that requires thinking because you aren't up to coping with any challenges. Do you see yourself as getting the job? Do you think such a statement would enhance your employability in the other person's eyes?

Turn that around: Picture yourself making a similar declaration about your inability to reason things through or to cope with difficulty to a prospective fiancee, a new friend, a team coach. What do you see as their reaction? Would it be favorable? Would it be likely to solidify the relationship?

Now imagine you can declare with complete veracity that your thinking smarts are so polished that all you have to do is look at a problem and you can spot the most logical answer virtually every time. How do you see potential employers and friends responding? Would it be the same? It's a statement the logical intelligence section of this program will enable you to make with confidence.

Learn to exercise your thinking smarts and you be able to:

- Switch your logical thinking processes on with the speed of a 1,000 megahertz-processor.

- Leapfrog quickly to the right solution or the correct explanation for any problem by applying "problem-busting" logic.

- Troubleshoot your own mental processes until they are error free with "zero defect" thinking.

- Develop a nose for anything that doesn't make sense, instantly detecting logical errors, flawed data, and attempts at misrepresentation in reports, speeches, statistics, explanations, and arguments.

- Become a math wizard; do sums and totals in your head at a glance.

THREE PROVEN STRATEGIES FOR UNLOCKING YOUR LOGICAL IQ

As you expand your thinking smarts, you may find the following to be enjoyable ways of keeping them flexible and at their optimum:

1. *Allow yourself ample time to answer questions asked or problems posed.* Snap judgments are seldom productive judgments. Gather all the relevant evidence you can, take the time to understand, deliberate, and ponder it. Then you will feel secure your answer is as sound as it can possibly be.

2. *Ask open-ended questions that leave room for the possibility that there is more than one right answer.* When we assume there is only one right solution to any problem, we often discard ideas that point the way toward alternative answers. Knowing there is more than one right answer to problems frees you to suggest and act on solutions without being afraid you will look foolish by coming up with the "wrong" answer.

3. *Keep your logical IQ active* by watching science, court, and business programs on television, visiting museums, taking a science class, or touring plants and factories that manufacture high-tech products.

PUTTING THE POWER OF THINKING TO WORK FOR YOU

Days 8 to 11 will leave you with no reason to feel bashful about your thinking smarts. Four powerful easy-to-follow mental strategies will help you super-size your logical intelligence.

EXERCISE: PROBLEM BUSTING

Sometimes it seems problems, disasters, and mental challenges follow one another in endless procession. As Gilda Radner's character says on *Saturday Night Live* reruns, "It's always something." Or, as Forrest Gump said, "Sh-t happens."

And, when it does, who you gonna call? Certainly not "Problem-busters." Dan Ackroyd, Bill Murray, and Winston Zeddemore aren't going to appear in white uniforms and magically hose your troubles away.

Confronted by a critical decision or a difficult situation you must puzzle through, you have only three options: (1) deal with it yourself; (2) hope someone else will solve it for you; (3) do nothing and breathe a sigh of relief if things happen to work out in your favor on their own or suffer the consequences if they don't.

You probably won't be surprised to learn that people who become vice president of the European Marketing Division, win citations for best-run school meal plan, found a successful business, earn a medical degree, land that "impossible" client, find a way to pay off crushing debts, or purchase a boat and sail around the world all choose option one.

Far too many of us, however, muddle along with choices two and three, unaware that our hidden genius for logic could easily solve any problem, conundrum, or difficulty, if we would just turn the key and unlock it.

HOW ONE MAN SOLVED A PROBLEM AND BECAME AN INTERNATIONAL SUCCESS

I often ask audiences if they feel they have fulfilling jobs that match their background and interests. From a count of hands, it appears that 70 percent or more do not. Then I ask how many believe they could find such a position through using simple logic alone? Not so surprisingly, the same hands tend to be raised both times. I then tell them the story of a man who achieved success by doing nothing, using simple logic to solve this problem and find himself the ideal job.

Shortly after the end of World War II, a gangling, bespectacled young man named Forrest James Ackerman, recently demobilized, along with hundreds of thousands of other American soldiers, from the U.S. Army Corps, sat down in a rented room in Los Angeles to take stock of his peacetime fate. He wanted something more than a routine job as a clerk or as jerking soda in a pharmacy—but what?

Ackerman possessed a degree in English and had a wide-ranging knowledge of books and magazines obtained as an omnivorous reader, plus an impeccable sense of spelling and grammar. On the whole, a career in some aspect of publishing and literature seemed called for.

One possibility was becoming an editor, but New York was already crowded with editors, and he would have to move there (away from the scene of his other passion: movies). Ackerman considered writing, as he'd already sold a few stories, but none of them were world-beaters and there were so many truly talented authors. Finally, there was the literary-agent game, a job that required the ability to recognize a good manuscript and a familiarity with magazines and book publishers, both of which Ackerman felt he had. Becoming a literary agent possessed another plus: You didn't have to move to Manhattan to practice it. You could run a literary agency from anywhere in the country.

But Ackerman recognized that there were other agents, and that he needed something to make him stand out. At the time, most agents covered the whole spectrum of literature: nonfiction fiction, mystery, western, romance, sports. Ackerman determined to become a specialist. He would limit his agency to form of literature he enjoyed most and knew best: science fiction.

It was a timely move, for science fiction was just breaking out of the pulp ghetto and gaining respectability. As the first agent to actively seek science fiction writers, Ackerman found himself an almost overnight success, with a host of now celebrated clients including blossoming young talents such as Ray Bradbury.

Eventually, as a result of the success he achieved through finding the answer to his problem, Ackerman would achieve renown in all the careers he had been forced to pass over. His fame as a science fiction specialist led to invitations to edit science fiction anthologies and write books about the genre. Through marketing movie rights to his clients' works, Ackerman became more deeply involved with the film industry, which resulted in opportunities to rewrite and write science fiction films. A publisher, aware of Ackerman's extensive knowledge of science fiction films, hired him to produce a magazine devoted wholly to the subject. (Ackerman even coined the term, "sci-fi.")

Now, I ask you, does any of the thinking involved in Ackerman's answering the question of what kind of profession might suit him best sound difficult or esoteric? Typically, after I have described the mental process that made him a success, audiences look bored or disappointed. It sounds elementary, like child's play to most people. It's the kind of thinking they do all the time. Is that all there is to problem solving, they want to know?

Yes, that is basically all there is to problem solving, I reply. That, a bit of training, a healthy dose of conscious, daily exercise, and what Richard Paul of the Foundation for Critical Thinking calls a willingness to tackle problems and not "dismiss a problem if it appears too complex."

HOW TO REDUCE A MOUNTAIN OF A PROBLEM INTO A MOLEHILL IN SIX EASY STEPS

There are many types of problems, and this can make solving problems seem more intimidating. It's natural to suppose that each type of dilemma ought to require a different approach to solve it. But this is another instance of appearances being deceiving. Though there are dozens, perhaps hundreds, of different categories and orders of dilemmas, the same six-step process solves them all.

All six steps played a part in Ackerman's process of putting two and two together to pinpoint the best career. (If they don't become apparent as you review these steps, you will find them given in detail in the logical intelligence builder exercise, "Problem-Busting," following.) You can use it to find an answer to even the biggest, most challenging problems. These six steps are

1. Identifying the question or problem

2. Identifying what you hope to accomplish by solving it

3. Reviewing the facts or evidence

4. Asking yourself what makes sense (using open-ended questions that don't imply there is only one solution)

5. Identifying what seems the most sensible answer and trying it to see if it works

6. If the solution doesn't work, reviewing your thinking and going with what seems the next most sensible solution

Amazingly, the odds are better than ten to one—in your favor—that the solution you think sensible enough to try first will work. According to research in educational testing, when people second-guess themselves and change their answers on tests, their first answer turns out to have been right in about ten out of eleven cases.

LOGICAL INTELLIGENCE BUILDER: PROBLEM-BUSTING

You have all the thinking smarts you need to find the answer to any difficulty. This practical, easy-to-learn exercise will show you how to switch on this portion of your brain power at will.

1. *Identify the question you must answer or the problem you must resolve.* Write it down in a sentence or two. (In the case of Forrest Ackerman, he might have written, "Find the ideal peacetime job for someone with my capabilities.")

2. *Identify why you need to solve it.* Write down your overall purpose. Here are some hints: What is the outcome you are trying to bring about? Why is the situation undesirable? What would have to happen to make it desirable? (Ackerman might have written, "Army life wasn't desirable, as it did not match my background or engage my interests. I want a job that does both.")

3. *Review the evidence, thinking about the elements of the problem.* Look for patterns. Ask yourself, What seems most relevant? What seems least relevant? What seems to go together? What doesn't? Jot down your conclusions in these areas in a sentence or two each. (Ackerman might have written, "Literary background and interests. Don't want to move to New York. Like movies. Knowledgeable in science fiction, know almost all writers, editors, publishers, etc.")

4. *Ask yourself, considering the problem and evidence, what makes sense?* What does the evidence suggest? Are there any clues to a solution? Remember to use open-ended questions that don't imply there is only one right answer and to generate several possible solutions. If logic fails to suggest the solution, try brainstorming how it can be achieved, or ask others for input. Write down three or four alternative answers in a sentence or two each. (Ackerman might have written, "Could be writer, especially sci-fi, but not so talented. Not hard-shelled enough to be producer or director. Very qualified to be editor or publisher, particularly of that genre. Also qualified as literary agent."

5. *Pick what seems the most sensible solution and try it.* Take a moment to review and compare the possible solutions you have written down. Ask, Which seems most supported by the evidence? Which seems to make the most sense? Which seems most likely to work given all the evidence? Write it down, and then implement it. (Ackerman might have written, "Not moving to New York rules out becoming editor or publisher. Lack of talent rules out writer. Leaves agent—agents can live wherever they like. Sci-fi is getting big—might specialize in sci-fi.")

6. *If your first solution should fail to work, review steps 1-5, ask yourself if your previous thinking still makes sense.* If so, try what seems your second most logical solution. If not, write down what you believe was the mistake, and any new options that occur to you. Then implement what seems the next most logical answer. (In Ackerman's case, he hit pay dirt right off the bat, becoming an overnight success as a literary agent with a stable of sci-fi luminaries.

But, if he hadn't, he might have reviewed his thinking and decided the agency idea was sound, but that his focus was too narrow, and would have broadened his stable to include writers from other fields of literature. Or, he might have reconsidered relocating to New York and sought a position as editor. Or he might have noticed he overlooked the possibility of working in the story department of a movie studio, reviewing scripts for producers and directors. Any of these might also have brought success.)

At first look, this can be a deceptively simple exercise. But the results can be eye-opening. Give these six steps a try, and with a little practice, you will find this process becoming automatic. On lesser problems, you won't be aware of it. All these steps will take place in your unconscious, virtually instantaneously, and the answer will just pop into your mind, seemingly without conscious effort on your part. Eventually, you will be able to switch on your logical intelligence faster than the world's fastest CPU.

THE POWER TECHNIQUE YOU'LL LEARN TOMORROW

Lose your fear of making mistakes. The next step of the logical intelligence portion of the super brain power program presents a technique for troubleshooting your own thinking processes to eliminate mistakes and produce "zero-defect thinking."

EXERCISE: ZERO-DEFECT THINKING

"To err is human, to forgive, divine." The phrase has been famous ever since it was coined in the early eighteenth century by poet Alexander Pope, perhaps because it was such a universal truism. The three pounds of gray matter that make up the brain are capable of many feats, but error-free operation isn't one of them.

Making decisions and living to regret them is an all too human trait. Whether it's that indiscreet remark at the office party, choosing the wrong mutual fund to invest in, or an unfortunate marriage, we've all made more than one choice we lived to sorrow over later. But you don't need to lose one more minute grieving over choices gone wrong.

Today takes yesterday's lesson in problem solving one step further and introduces you to "zero-defect thinking," a user-friendly exercise for double-checking your logical processes to make certain they are sound. I call it "zero-defect thinking" because it quickly shifts out and erases your mental lapses. With this technique you can hold a mental microscope up to anyone's thinking—your own and that of others—sifting out the most minute errors.

Zero-defect thinking empowers the best in your thinking, freeing it to emerge while winnowing away the chaff. It liberates you to act with confidence. You have the certainty of knowing you have eliminated all possible mistakes, missteps, and misjudgments, have reached the best possible decision, and are capable of solving any other problems that arise along the way.

The ability to act with confidence is often cited as an essential characteristic of those who succeed in life. As "the world's greatest salesman," Joe Girard, who devotes an entire chapter to "Self-confidence" in *Mastering Your Way to the Top*, says, "Confidence is the muscle that lets you tackle risk-taking and win. Confidence is the daily bench press that beefs up your ability to overcome obstacles, and puts muscle in your self-assurance."

This kind of confidence in your decision making can be yours. Once unlocked, the power of your logical intelligence to catch "glitches" will quickly give you reason to have faith in your own mental processes. As with all the techniques in this book, a little practice releases a large portion of brain power.

THE MISSING STEP THAT TURNS LOSERS INTO WINNERS

Victor had inherited a small company that manufactured orthopedic shoes. It wasn't a position he wanted, but family obligations forced him to step into the presidency.

Victor, who had just squeezed through business school, didn't feel he was promising managerial material. He considered himself a muddy thinker who avoided making decisions. Otherwise, he would have stood up to his father and gone to a teacher's college rather than to business school.

The situation Victor was plunged into realized his fears. The company was profitable, but faced growing threats from abroad. Various family members—uncles, aunts, brothers, and sisters—owned portions of the business, and they were always squabbling over how things ought to be done.

Decisions were demanded of Victor practically on the hour around the clock. He hated making them and kept putting them off. Victor was out of his depth and couldn't cope. But in a way, Victor was already a genius. He knew he couldn't cope and needed to do something about it.

So he booked a membership at a self-empowerment seminar that seemed exactly what the doctor ordered. Its focus was on executives who experienced difficulty making decisions. Or if they did reach one, who kept putting off acting on it afterward.

The seminar was led by a motivational superstar whose audio- and video-tape sets had sold millions through television infomercials. Using humor, anecdote, and a multimedia slide and video presentation, the motivation guru drilled Victor and other audience members in the basic steps of problem solving. He worked hard to inspire audience members with the confidence to begin making decisions they had been putting off—and to acting on those decisions—immediately after the seminar was over.

Victor left the event filled with conviction he could now think a problem through to its conclusion as well as anyone, and he determined to become a more decisive person. At work and at home, he confidently made choices and acted on them, once he had followed the basic steps and deliberated a matter thoroughly.

Most of Victor's decisions turned out right, and things began to run more smoothly at the office and in family interactions. But, every once in a while, one of his decisions would go wrong. And since he was simultaneously juggling a beleaguered company and a fractious family, the few "clunkers" cost him disproportionately, emotionally and financially.

Through a mutual friend, Victor asked me if the failures were an indication of his innate lack of intelligence or because he had misunderstood the problem-solving process. I assured him that neither was the case. Instead, the motivation guru had simply left an essential element out of the equation.

Even in mathematics, adding two and two together to get four does not quite complete the process. When we were taught math in school, the first caution the instructor offered was to go back over every problem and double-check it to be certain we hadn't misread a number, mistaken a plus for a minus, or added the total wrong. I e-mailed Victor a copy of the same exercise that follows.

According to our mutual acquaintance, as a result of applying his brain power this way, Victor's mistakes have been few and far between since then.

THE MOST IMPORTANT LESSON ANYONE CAN LEARN

At the start of every flight, pilot and copilot are required to fill out a list several pages long, checking each instrument one at a time to make sure it is working, before the plane can be cleared for takeoff. Before a circus aerialist treads the tightwire high above the audience's heads, she and an assistant personally inspect every supporting post, every knot of the rigging, every inch of rope and wire. When you are driving in dense traffic, alert to signs of potential danger from drivers on the road ahead, you also glance in your rearview mirror occasionally to make sure there are no potentially dangerous drivers coming up from behind you. You don't just purchase a business based on the owner's evaluation; you talk to the owner's bankers, customers, and creditors first.

Moral: Having the confidence to solve problems and make decisions is at least half the battle. The other half is double-checking your thinking before acting, or afterward if things go wrong. Learning this simple lesson is often what spells the difference between those who make their lifetime dreams reality and those who never quite do.

General George Pickett reached what seemed a reasonable decision that legendary day in 1863 and acted decisively upon it. The results of "Pickett's charge" can be found in any history book that includes the U.S. Civil War. It included a decisive loss for the South (25,000 Confederate soldiers dead or wounded), which lacked the population and troops to recover. But if Pickett had paused to double-check his thinking and had avoided his disastrous charge, the South might have succeeded in its invasion of the North, capturing not only the Union's capital, but the Union's leader, Abraham Lincoln, as well.

Every one of millions of circuits, pipelines, fuel chambers, computer routines, and other elements must function perfectly or a space shuttle mission is scrubbed, even if it is sitting on the launch pad with everyone aboard and the engines already warmed and smoking. That's one reason there haven't been any further shuttle fatalities since the *Challenger.*

Not to belabor the point, but so many people seem to omit this all-important step, that it's worth repeating. Sometimes, a few minutes spent exercising your logical IQ, by way of troubleshooting your thinking processes, can reveal errors and save you from courses of actions that could have proved disastrous if followed.

THREE STEPS TO ZERO-DEFECT THINKING

Educators call this process of double-checking your problem-solving skills "critical thinking." Psychologists call it "metacognition." Others have described this facet of your logical intelligence as "thinking about thinking."

Thinking about thinking may seen like a brain-twisting concept. But, as educator Edmund Hartley, Ph.D., writes, it's nothing more than "examining one's reasoning processes to evaluate their appropriateness and effectiveness." It's another of those innate capacities of your logical IQ, and the one ability that really does appear to set us apart from animals.

Today's exercise, zero-defect thinking, shows how you can draw on this aspect of your thinking smarts to unlock three dynamic mental powers that will enable you to

- Double-check your own thinking before trying a solution, to reduce the likelihood of mistakes

- Double-check your own thinking when a solution fails to produce the desired result

- Double-check the ideas, arguments, and decisions of others

LOGICAL INTELLIGENCE BUILDER: ZERO-DEFECT THINKING

You can use this technique before acting on a decision to double-check your reasoning. It is also essential afterward, if anything has gone amiss and a decision has not worked out as well as you anticipated. The result will be to reduce errors in logic and reason to almost nothing.

I'll show you how it might be applied, from my own experience. I came to work for a publisher of medical self-help and recovery books. Their previous bestsellers had included titles on stress, asthma, arthritis, and heart conditions.

They had just experienced their first failure—a book on herpes. No one could understand what might have gone awry. The book's cover emulated the format of all their best-selling books, which seemed a winner, even to the uninitiated. The title of each book was the name of the illness, say, stress, printed in gigantic letters that almost filled the cover, with a small subtitle such as "ten steps to healing" in small type underneath it. It certainly seemed the ideal way to let people with those conditions know that the subject of this book was right down their alley. At a troubleshooting meeting I attended later, the publishing committee analyzed its error somewhat in the manner described here.

1. *Double-check your formulation of the problem.* Ask yourself, Is your understanding of the problem realistic? Have you defined it clearly? For what obstacle, difficulty, or unfulfilled need are you seeking a positive resolution? (At first glance, the publisher's formulation of the problem seemed reasonable: Design the book jacket that will attract attention of those who need it, in order to sell the most possible copies.)

2. *Double-check your formulation for possible biases.* What assumptions is it based on? How could these affect your understanding of the problem? Were alternative formulations of the issue considered? (The publisher's assumption was that what had worked on the covers of previous books about medical conditions would work on their herpes book, as well.)

3. *Double-check that the evidence supports your solution.* Was the evidence unbiased and accurate? Was it applied consistently and fairly? Was it truly relevant? (Their evidence, previous sales records, was reliable and fair. As to whether it was relevant, a marketing postmortem on the book admitted that these figures might not have been as applicable as they thought. None of their previous medical self-help titles had been about communicable conditions that could be cured or alleviated. None were communicable, and none carried a social stigma.)

4. *Double-check your reasons for deciding on the solution, outcome, or resolution you chose.* Does the evidence support it? What assumptions are implied by it? Are these clear and reasonable? Are they consistent with each other? (What the publisher realized, too late, was that the evidence may not have supported the conclusion.)

6. *Double-check the expected outcome.* What are the short-term and long-term consequences of applying this solution? Are they significant enough to warrant implementing it? Are they realistic? Have both negative and positive possibilities been considered? (One negative consequence the publisher realized they had not considered was that because herpes is a communicable disease, people who have it do not like to broadcast this fact. By making the word "herpes" so big on the cover, purchasing the book at a sales counter became the equivalent of announcing to everyone who worked for the store and all the other customers there that the purchaser most likely had this communicable disease. As a result, readers stayed away in droves.)

Had the publisher taken this into consideration they might have creatively reversed their cover formula and printed the subtitle "Five Steps to Health" in capital letters that nearly filled the cover, and might have printed the words "for those suffering from herpes" in small type at the bottom. Those searching for a book on herpes would have found it anyway in the health section of the bookstore. But, they wouldn't have had to feel they were broadcasting their condition to everyone.

According to critical thinking experts, in time following these six steps will also deepen your ability to see beneath the surface, understand alternative viewpoints, avoid being unduly influenced by what others say, decide what you think and why, and defend and adapt your positions intelligently.

THE POWER TECHNIQUE YOU'LL LEARN TOMORROW

Now it's time to super-size your logical intelligence and build on your newfound talent for troubleshooting your own thinking to catch others when they attempt to fool you with bogus logic. With the genius tomorrow's exercise unlocks, no one will ever again convince you black is white or pull the wool over your eyes by twisting the facts to conceal deception, lies, misleading arguments, phony statistics, and other hidden agendas.

Day 10 _____
EXERCISE: SPOTTING BOGUS LOGIC

Have you ever . . . been fooled into purchasing something that wasn't what you thought because of false advertising? . . . voted for a politician only to have him slither out of his announced positions later by pointing to carefully split hairs in his speeches? . . . signed a contract carefully worded to mislead you about the significance of certain clauses that came back to haunt you later? . . . let a business associate talk you into a course of action that appeared to make sense at the time but that turned out disastrously? . . . been cheated outright of money or property by someone with a great line of gab who deliberately twisted the facts to deceive and dupe you?

If you have been the victim of an individual or organization that manipulated the facts to manipulate you—it ends today! Never again will anyone throw dust in your eyes with false logic and convince you something makes sense when it doesn't. No one can pull the mental wool over your eyes if you are already wise to the seven basic subterfuges (or mental "traps") people use to make bogus logic look genuine so they can cheat and mislead others.

"A fool and his money are soon parted," is an old truism. The same could be said of votes, love, even jobs. Those who don't know when they are being manipulated are often the first to find themselves shut out in life.

Your logical intelligence has built-in antennae that can detect deliberately misleading logic, if properly and frequently exercised. Today's exercise super-sizes your thinking smarts by showing you the seven mental tricks people use to trap you into believing nonsense is sense and vice-versa. Like Mr. Spock on *Star Trek*, the minute someone tries to mislead you with bogus logic, you'll be able to say, "It does not compute!"

HOW ONE P.A. SPOTTED BOGUS LOGIC AND SAVED HER BOSS SIX FIGURES

Lucinda was a brilliant, exquisitely groomed young woman who worked as personal assistant to the world-famous head of a major cosmetics company. Lucinda's boss was a collector of fossils—the older and rarer the better. Her boss's collection consisted of rare, one-of-a-kind pieces, many of which should have been in museums or in the hands of paleontologists (scientists who study prehistoric animal life), but, alas, had knowingly been purchased on the black market.

Lucinda and her boss were at an industry conference in Rio de Janeiro when they received a visit from a dealer in antiquities they had done business with before. He had something very unusual to offer, he said, the only fossil ever discovered of a rare species of prehistoric insect known to have existed 200 million years ago. The antiquities dealer proffered a number of items in proof of the fossil's authenticity. There was a letter from an MIT-geologist who had visited the site days after the fossil was discovered. He detailed the exhaustive tests he and other scientists had done, proving that the layer of rock where the fossil had been found was 200 million years old. There was another letter from an equally distinguished entomologist who attested that photos of the fossil corresponded exactly to computer simulations of what the prehistoric insect would have looked like. There was even a third letter from a chemical laboratory certifying that the material of the fossil had been tested and was of the correct composition and age.

Lucinda's boss was eager to purchase the item for her collection. She felt she had found a priceless treasure any museum, collector, or paleontologist would kill for. The antiquities dealer had named a price high into six figures, and she hadn't even blinked.

Then Lucinda, whose judgment her employer had learned she could rely on, gave a signal they had worked over the years she had been the woman's personal assistant. Her boss looked annoyed, shook her head, and returned to concluding the deal. But when Lucinda gave the signal a second time, her boss slowed down and fended the man off, saying the price was so steep she wanted to think about it overnight.

What Lucinda pointed out after the antiquities dealer had left caused her boss to take certain actions, after which the fossil was exposed as a fraud. (Lucinda received a significant honorarium for her timely intervention.) How could this be? With three experts of unimpeachable character having authenticated the item with every possible test.

If you can't guess the answer, then today's exercise is a must. You'll learn to expand your brain power in this crucial arena by identifying the seven kinds of traps purveyors of bogus logic can lay for you. (By the way, if you haven't worked it out by then, you will find the answer to how Lucinda spotted the antique dealer's bogus logic explained in detail at the end of the logical intelligence builder, "Spotting Bogus Logic.")

HOW BOGUS LOGIC FOOLS YOU

On a recent visit to New York, I saw the old confidence game, Three-Card Monty, being played. This is a time-honored method of swindling gullible people of their money. In it, the operator places a court card and two number cards face down on a table, mixes them up, and bets twenty dollars of his own money against anyone who puts up five dollars that they can't pick the court card. It looks easy, when you see the three cards being switched around.

The catch is that you can't win; the game is a cheat. None of the three cards are the face card. The operator has used what magicians call "sleight-of-hand" to palm the face card and substitute a number card in the process of mixing up the cards. If anyone catches on and accuses him of this, he apparently proves the game is honest by turning the remaining two cards face up (resubstituting the face card for the number card in what seems the simple act of flipping it over).

Three-Card Monty is a variant of a method that has been used for duping the credulous that goes back at least as far as Egypt and Mesopotamia. It originally involved three walnut-shell halves (or small clay cups) and a kernel of corn. Again, the operator used sleight of hand to cheat players out of their money by removing the pea invisibly while mixing the shells around.

In a similar way, some people use what you can think of as sleight of thinking to defraud, deceive, bluff, and manipulate you for their own advantage. Sleight of thinking is a fancy way of saying bogus logic. It's a method of deliberately putting words and facts together so they appear to mean one thing but actually mean another, or appear to make sense when they really don't. You are tricked into believing there is a kernel of reason in what they say, but in fact, their entire argument is as bogus and empty as those Mesopotamian walnut shells.

Bogus logic and sleight of thinking are more formally known by academics under the name "fallacy." You probably learned about fallacies in high school or freshman college. Fallacies are special ways of bending reasoning to flimflam others, so that what seems a model of logical thought turns out later—like a house sold by an unscrupulous landlord—to have holes in the foundation and inadequate support for the roof.

And just as there are only about five or six basic sleight-of-hand tricks, which con artists and stage magicians adapt to a wide variety of illusions, so there are only seven basic kinds of bogus logic that can be used to gull the unwary in a multitude of ways. Since you learned to catch your own twisted thinking with yesterday's exercise, when you learn to catch attempts to deliberately twist your thinking it's almost like doubling that gain in brain power again.

THE SEVEN MENTAL TRAPS OF BOGUS LOGIC

Like the tricks of con men and magicians, what makes bogus logic work is distraction. Your attention is diverted from faulty thinking by irrelevant or emotionally charged elements. Sleight of thinking is used to distract you from the obvious failure to make sense. Fortunately, your logical intelligence is up to the challenge of recognizing the seven mental traps of bogus logic. These are:

1. *False dilemma.* To dissuade you from a course, misleadingly suggests all the consequences will be negative, while there are actually positive possibilities as well. For example, "This new business deal will either drive us out of business or ruin our standing in our field."

2. *Appeal to authority.* *(In school this was known as argu-mentum ad verecundiam.)* Takes two key forms:

- *Citing an expert.* Tricks you into believing a statement because an impressive authority supports it. Being an expert doesn't make one right, however, as many times experts in a field disagree. A few years ago two respected physicists claimed to have discovered "cold fusion." Other physicists doubted it. They were right; the two men had falsified their research.

- *Citing a celebrity.* A famous expert is said to support an idea, but there's a catch—he isn't an expert in the same field. For example, "Donald Trump says the best social policy is benign neglect." He may know about real estate, but not about gov-erning.

3. *Playing on sympathy.* (In school, *argumentum ad misericor-diam.)* You are tricked into overlooking an idea's weakness by a mov-ing description of some unfortunate's plight. For example, "Thirty million school children don't get a nutritious lunch. Vote for this plan, and they will." The thought of millions of malnourished children is calculated to distract you from the plan's defects.

4. *Attacking the messenger.* (In school, *argumentum ad hominem.)* Takes two main forms:

- *Attacking the messengers' character.* Suggests anything they say should be rejected because of their morals, competency, nationality, or religion. For example, "I don't care what Senator Jones says about taxation, he got caught with his secretary."

- *Attacking the messengers' acquaintances.* Suggests anything they say is unreliable because they have unreliable associates. For example, "You can't believe a word Jesus says. He's always hanging around in dockside taverns with prostitutes and drunkards."

5. *It happened afterward; that proves a connection.* (In school, *post hoc ergo propter hoc.)* Claims one thing caused another merely because it happened first. For example, "Ever since I began using computers I've had an itch. The radiation from the computer must be causing my itch."

6. *False generalizations.* Leaps to conclusions on too little or inapplicable evidence. Takes two forms.

- Hasty generalizations. Leaping to a conclusion based on minimal knowledge (which might not turn out to be accurate) before weighing all the evidence. For example, "My six best friends thought my idea of a nose mitten was great, so everyone will want to buy it."

- *Sweeping generalizations.* (In school, *dicto simplicter.*) Leaping to a conclusion by applying a general rule to an incompatible situation. For example, "I've heard that part of town is dangerous. I wouldn't deliver that package." The street in question might be the safest in the city.

7. *False comparison.* To confuse the issue, the argument is based on two things that aren't comparable but are spoken of as if they were. For example, "Workers are like horses. You have to keep horses under control or they run wild, and you have to keep employees under control or they'll run wild, too."

LOGICAL INTELLIGENCE BUILDER: SPOTTING BOGUS LOGIC

When you first begin exercising your brain power by spotting sleight of thinking, this checklist will help you remember the seven basic traps of bogus logic. Once you achieve proficiency, you won't need to rely on the checklist any longer. The process will become natural and automatic.

You'll be inoculated against attempts to infect your thinking with bogus logic. People will never again take advantage of you with deceptive arguments designed to distract you from their failure to make sense. Your thinking smarts are more than sufficient to catch anyone engaging in slight-of-thinking, if you just look for:

❏ *False dilemma.* Ask yourself, is the main support for not doing this that only negative outcomes have been cited?

❏ *The two forms of appeal to authority.*

- Look for citing an expert. Ask yourself, is the main support for this an authority's endorsement?

- Citing a celebrity. Ask yourself, is the main support for this a famous expert, but from a different field?

❏ *Appeals to sympathy.* Ask yourself, is the main support for this the moving description of a pitiable condition?

❏ *The two forms of attack on the messenger.*

- Attacks on the messenger's character. Ask yourself, is the main argument against this an attack on someone's morals, competency, nationality, or religion?

- Attacks on the messenger's acquaintances. Ask yourself, is the main argument against believing this that a supporter has unreliable associates?

❏ *It happened afterward, that proves a connection.* Ask yourself, is the main reason for believing this is the cause merely because it happened first?

❏ *The two forms of false generalizations.*

- Hasty generalization. Ask yourself, is the main support for this a conclusion based on a small or preliminary sampling of knowledge that could turn out later to be misrepresentative?

- Sweeping generalization. Ask yourself, is the main support for this the application of a general rule to a specific situation where it doesn't apply?

❏ *False comparison.* Ask yourself, is the main support for this an analogy between two things that aren't comparable, but are spoken of as if they were?

(By now you may have guessed the specific type of bogus logic Lucinda spotted. It was citing a celebrity—three times over. Each of the authorities, the geologist, entomologist, and chemist was an expert. But not in fossils themselves. The antiquities dealer had deliberately avoided the one kind of expert who could have pronounced unequivocally on the fossil's authenticity, a paleontologist. When Lucinda pointed this out, her boss had the fossil examined by such an expert, who pronounced it a clever forgery. But, here's the kicker: It had been cleverly carved by a professional art forger out of a much larger, but common and valueless, fossil of the right age, one that would pass all the tests put to it by experts outside the field.)

THE POWER TECHNIQUE YOU'LL LEARN TOMORROW

If I had told you earlier that tomorrow you will learn to become a math wizard, you probably would have scoffed, to say the least. But now that you have experienced the powers of your logical IQ to solve problems and detect fallacy, you may be ready to believe my promise that tomorrow's exercise will give a boost to your arithmetical skills.

Day 11 _____

EXERCISE: MATH WIZARDRY

Today's exercise takes your newly expanded thinking smarts and shows you how to combine them with some powerful strategies to help you become a genius at arithmetic. This is another of those super brain power abilities that, unless you were lucky enough to be a whiz at math in school, you probably won't believe is possible until you have put it to the test for yourself. Yet, your logical intelligence is already high enough to do complicated addition, subtraction, and multiplication in your head without benefit of paper and pen.

You probably thought math was about things like the multiplication tables. And since you had trouble remembering those, especially the hard ones such as 7 times 8, you probably concluded that you were a blockhead when it came to math and pretty much gave up on it as soon as you were out of school.

But, frankly, the good old multiplication tables turn out not to be very relevant to most real-life math problems, whether you use a pen and paper or not. Let's say you are purchasing 36 reams (500 sheets) of paper for your boss at 89 cents per ream. That's 36 times 89. Where are your multiplication tables then? They're great if you are multiplying one digit by another digit, but not much use when the numbers go to two digits and beyond.

When that happens, you have to multiply the top figure by the right-hand number below, carry numbers, and add them up. Then you multiply the top figure by the left-hand number below, carry and add and finally add the two totals. That's a bit taxing for people to do in their head.

So let's simplify things and add 1 to that 89 to make it 90. That's a simple figure and a simple one to work with. It's probably easy for you to multiply 90 by 36 in your head and come up with 3,240. Now, since we added an additional 36 to that 89 to simplify things and make it 90, we need to subtract that 36. Subtracting 36 from 3,240 isn't difficult. Without pen and paper you can still come up with 3,204. If they were charging $89 per ream, the total would be $1,869. But since the price was 89 cents, or $.89, we need to insert the two decimal points. Total price: $18.69.

HOW MATH WIZARDRY ENSURES SUCCESS

You can't get very far in the world if you are a dummy at math. The person who can stand up at an office meeting and confidently answer the new department head's question about what it will cost if they up the advertising budget by 47 percent is off to a flying start. The person who can listen to a telephone solicitor say, "Doesn't a year's subscription to *Better Woman's Journal* for only 13 cents a day sound great?" and think quickly—Thirteen cents a day is 91 cents, almost a dollar, per week. Times fifty-two weeks is 52 dollars. The magazine costs five dollars, times twelve issues per year is 60 dollars. Fifty-two dollars isn't such a good deal, after all, since most magazine subscriptions are one third or more off the sale price, or about 40 dollars per year—who won't be ripped off financially very often. People can glance through the day's stock market figures and know to within a percentage or two the value of their portfolio will never wake up one morning to find it has slowly evaporated without their noticing. People who can do sums mentally as fast as a cashier rings up their purchases at the supermarket will never be overcharged. People who can walk into a building they are considering leasing for their new company and quickly figure out the monthly price from cost per square foot will go far in business.

It's hard to imagine someone rising very far in any career or profession without some skill in math. Robert Townsend would never have become CEO of Avis Rent-a-Car if he had to take someone else's word for the figures on an important business deal. At the other end of the scale, try to imagine the average homemaker getting through the week on budget without being able to do the math to tell a real bargain from a come-on or knowing to within a dollar or less the total value of the items in his or her shopping cart. The importance of quick, in-your-head math skills to success in all aspects of daily life simply can't be overemphasized. Fortunately, you already have your own arithmetical genius on tap in the form of your logical intelligence. Today's exercise guides you through an almost effortless technique for enlisting this unexploited brain power in your behalf.

SEVEN MUST-HAVE MATH TALENTS THIS EXERCISE GIVES YOU

With the hidden genius the math wizardry technique unlocks you will gain the power to add, subtract, and multiply even complicated numbers in your head. You can expect to

- Total dinner bills and figure the tip instantly

- Catch mistakes in balance sheets, financial plans, and forecasts

- Keep running totals of investments, bank accounts, and 401(k)s in your head

- Spot overcharges as the store is ringing up the bill

- Follow intricate corporate balance sheets without difficulty

- Race through the creation of annual budgets and long-term financial planning

- Maintain meticulous expense accounts

HOW MATH WIZARDRY HELPED A PRODUCER OUT-ADD AN ACCOUNTANT

I was once asked to take over the helm as coproducer of a documentary call *Dreamspinner*, a tribute to *Twilight Zone* and *Star Trek* writer George Clayton Johnson. The project was being shot on a minuscule budget, and tight reigns had to be held on expenditures. At the end of each day's shooting, the accountant (who had an MA in math) and I would review an itemized list of each cost incurred. While he added it up laboriously on a calculator, I would do the sums mentally and finish far ahead of the accountant, with a total that was always within a few dollars of the actual figure.

Why? I'm not a math genius. Far from it. I received Bs, Cs, and even Ds in arithmetic, and nearly flunked algebra.

But my friend, the late spy novelist David McDaniel, taught me a few simple shortcuts for applying your figure smarts to addition, subtraction, and multiplication that most math geniuses don't know. They don't have a difficult time doing arithmetical problems in their heads, so they don't need shortcuts. But the rest of us do.

FOUR STEPS TO MATH WIZARDRY

The basics of math are easy. Anyone can add and subtract simple numbers like 2 plus 7 in their head. The difficulty enters when you add 36 to 28, or subtract 48 from 95, and you have leftover sums you have to "carry" or "borrow," like when you subtract 8 from 5 and borrow 1 from the 9 to make 8, and then take 8 from 15 to get 7, and 4 from (what was that number) to make what?

Math wizardry throws out all that complicated carrying and borrowing and breaks the problem down to simple addition and subtraction again. Instead of adding, say, 23 to 28, which can be tricky when you are doing the carrying in your head, it can be a lot easier and faster to simply add 23 to 30, for 53 and then subtract the 2 you added to get the 30.

As productivity consultant K. Thomas Finley writes in *Mental Dynamics*, "A few basic rules can enable you to solve most simple math problems in your head. And, happily, you don't have to be a mathematical marvel." Math wizardry is just that, four brain-easy rules that put your logical intelligence to working smarter, not harder.

These four rules are:

1. *When adding figures in your head* (say 38 and 64), to avoid carrying, change the figure ending in the highest digit (38) to the next highest number ending in zero (40). Then add that rounded figure (40) to the other number (64) to get the subtotal (104). Next, subtract the number you added to do the rounding off (2), for a final answer (102).

2. *When subtracting figures in your head* (say 54 from 98), to avoid borrowing, change figure you are subtracting (54) to the next highest number ending in zero (60). Then add the same amount (6) to the top figure (98) for a subtotal (104). Then subtract the rounded figure (60) from that figure (104) for a final answer (44).

3. *When multiplying figures in your head* (say 300 by 8,000), if both numbers end in zeros, multiply the first two numbers (3 times 8), then add to that answer (24) the total number of zeros in the numbers you multiplied (5) for a final answer (2,400,000).

4. *When multiplying difficult figures in your head* (say 25 by 34), break them down into two easier problems (say 20 times 34, and 5 times 34). Multiply the first problem (20 times 34, or 680), then the second (5 times 34, or 170). Next, add the two sums (680 plus 170) for a final answer (850).

Practice each of these simple techniques for a day or two, and you will find you have completely mastered this portion of your hidden genius.

THE POWER TECHNIQUE YOU WILL LEARN TOMORROW

If you think creativity is only for artists and doesn't have anything to do with you, the three days of exercises that begin tomorrow will open your eyes to your creative intelligence's awesome power to help make your life and endeavors a success.

.

The Fourth Key—

UNLOCKING YOUR CREATIVE GENIUS

WHAT'S YOUR CREATIVE IQ?

This test helps you form a rough estimate of your creative intelligence as it is at this moment. Don't judge yourself adversely if the test shows your idea smarts to be idling along at a low rate. Finish the first exercise (day 12) and watch how it shifts your score upward. Or if you feel in any way that lack of creativity is holding you back from moving forward in life or realizing a dream, these three days of the program will unlock the hidden well of genius you've longed to tap.

Check the box beside any description that feels as if it applies to you. Do you typically

- ❐ Experience a constant flow of original ideas in response to things you encounter or learn of during the course of a day?

- ❐ Find yourself struck, from time to time, by a sudden "flash" of insight when you've been "stuck" for an answer to a problem for a long time?

- ❐ Finish a bad television show or movie thinking you could have written or directed it better yourself?

- ❐ Adapt easily to changing circumstances and jobs?

- ❐ Fantasize and daydream constantly, picturing yourself in various real-life or motion-picture scenarios?

- ❐ Recall getting excellent marks in creative writing, art, or drama during your school years?

❑ Enjoy learning new skills, hobbies, sports, facts, philosophies, cultural perspectives, and points of view?

❑ Know intuitively, after hearing the first few words (or notes) of a new song how the rest of the chorus will go, or after reading the first few pages of a story know how it will end?

❑ See ways things could be rearranged to improve them?

❑ Have a vocation or avocation that involves the arts, from writing and painting to amateur dramatics, going to the movies, and visiting museums?

❑ Dress stylishly or colorfully?

❑ Fail more often than others because you are willing to take risks and try new things more often than others?

❑ Experience emotions more intently than do other people?

❑ Ask and think iconoclastic questions that challenge common assumptions and the way things are normally done?

❑ Have intense, full-color dreams that you remember when you wake up in the morning?

Scoring: Add up the number of boxes you checked.

If your score was between 1 and 4, these three days of exercises are your ticket to vastly increased creativity. You haven't been using your idea smarts—and it shows. You may hear a few "creaks" while you work the stiffness out, but you will soon find your brain becoming a fertile breeding ground for all kinds of novel and original concepts.

If your score was between 5 and 8, you're probably content with watching a good movie or television program and enjoying the fruits of other people's creative IQ. But you don't consider yourself to be creative, and so you infrequently attempt to use your own creativity. If that's your situation, the next few pages will be a revelation, leaving you with an inspired new vision of your idea smarts and how they can contribute to your overall success in life.

If your score was between 9 and 12, your creative IQ is in pretty good shape. At the least, you are someone who reads dozens of novels each year (and dreams of being a writer) or is a weekend painter of seascapes or wields the camcorder at family gatherings. With a head start like that, the three days dedicated to expanding creative intelligence will lift your idea smarts far enough to take you from amateur to professional standing.

If your score was between 13 and 15, there isn't much anyone can show you about how to use your creative intelligence. Your major contribution, wherever you work, is probably through your idea smarts. But, unless you already know about what science calls "ultradian rhythms" and the creative peak you hit every 90 to 120 minutes, this section may still hold a few surprises.

UNLOCKING YOUR CREATIVE INTELLIGENCE

Creativity, the ability to "brainstorm" new ideas and solutions, is the *sine qua non* of achieving one's goals, whatever they may be. Tom Peters, hailed by *Fortune* magazine as the "Ur-guru" (guru of gurus) of management, ranked "Number One among American business leaders" with a "Credibility Index" more than twice that of the runner-up, Bill Gates, singles out creativity as "the most important quality a leader can possess." Tony Robbins, creator of the Unlimited Power Program of best-selling audio- and videotapes, and Fortune 500 consultant, also ranks it as an essential for those who desire to "have, do, and achieve anything they want out of life."

That kind of creativity isn't the provenance of moguls and millionaires or artists and artisans alone. You possess the identical allocation of imagination and inventiveness, and the identical potential for using it to realize your own dreams. Creativity is what gets you through many of the day's problems, though you may have been so preoccupied—finding an alternate way to work now that the city's mass transit is out on strike and finding a way to get the day's summaries out after your assistant phoned in sick and arranging a nice evening for that rich uncle who's coming to town for the weekend—to see that creativity was involved at all.

Regardless of where your total fell in the creative IQ test (page 143), you not only *can* be more creative, you already *are* more creative than you think. Building on nothing more than your ability to accomplish scenarios such as the preceding ones, these three days of the super brain power program will help you lift your own creativity high enough to make any dream or any ambition—no matter how intimidating—a reality.

HOW YOU CAN BE A CREATIVE GENIUS

Our baby teeth aren't the only things we lose young. Our creativity apparently disappears when we are young, too. Children's drawings, stories, and play show creativity develops quickly in early childhood, according to professor Mark Runco, founder of the *Creativity Research Journal.* But tests show that by age seven, most of us lose the creative urge. Apparently, it takes only about a year in the educational system to discourage grade schoolers (and the adults they later become) from relating to their creative IQs.

This loss of creative intelligence is not very surprising, says Mark Runco, considering what happens to children in the school system. "We put children in groups and make them sit in desks and raise their hands before they talk. We put all the emphasis on conformity and order, then we wonder why they aren't being spontaneous and creative."

A second factor that cuts most of us off from our idea smarts is that we assume creative people must have enormous IQs, and since our IQs aren't all that high, we further assume that we can't be all that creative. But it turns out that highly successful authors, painters, musicians, scientists, business people, and other creative types are no smarter than anyone else.

Psychology professor Dean Simonton, Ph.D., has conducted hundreds of experiments into creativity, but has been unable to establish any kind of relationship between it and intelligence. According to Simonton, you don't have to be a genius to be a creative genius. Most are no smarter than anyone else.

As David Henry Feldman, a developmental psychologist who conducts creativity studies at Tufts University, puts it, "All humans, by virtue of being dreamers and fantasizers, are creative. They are always transforming their inner and outer worlds."

CREATIVITY: YOUR LIFE PRESERVER IN ROUGH TIMES

Until now, you probably assumed you weren't creative, that your job entering data in an insurance office, or taking applications at the registry of motor vehicles, or running the machine that copies three dozen videocassettes at a time, or as a homemaker, or grading real estate examination papers, or inspecting newly installed wiring for the city has nothing to do with creativity. You probably assumed it's strictly for people with jobs in advertising, entertainment media, the arts, perhaps the most rarefied of executive suites, and other creative-type professions.

But creativity lies behind many a success, from the prosaic and mundane through the sublime, from how to plug the hole in your car's radiator hose long enough to limp to the nearest garage, to the imaginative proposal that wins the hoped-for response of "Yes, I will marry you," to the 3 A.M. inspiration that allows you to walk into City Hall Monday morning with the answer to the problem of widening the Old City Bridge without disrupting traffic to the foundering mall on the other side that has just invested millions in renovation.

Apple Computers is one long story of creative inspirations (with only a minor interregnum when Steve Jobs was not at the helm), beginning with the user-friendly graphics and icons that won so many people to Macintosh (and from Windows to PCs), and continuing with the astounding success of Job's newest inspiration, the cheerful, colorful IMAC. Creativity is what got Steve Case through the rough spots when they were negotiating the Time-Warner–AOL merger.

For that matter, your own innate creativity is the life preserver that gets you through the rough spots in your life. The rough spots in life aren't necessarily when something goes wrong or you are faced with difficulty. The rough patches are when you don't know how to get things back on course or resolve the difficulty. Most of the time, we know what to do when the car breaks down or a manager drops an extra task on our desk with a near impossible deadline.

It's the times when you have tried everything you know of that's worked before and none of it works—when you need a new angle or approach—that your idea smarts kick in and get you through. Creativity has carried humankind from the cave to the condo and through all the rough patches in between. Other animals may see or smell or hear or use tools as well as humans, but none are within leagues of us in creativity.

Creativity is so central a part of our makeup as human beings that unlike the other intelligences, it isn't confined to one area of the brain. Instead, the brain complexes that constitute your creative intelligence extend throughout, and draw on, *all* the other intelligences (and many other regions of the brain, as well).

So there is no chance you are suffering from any shortage of idea smarts. We've all been richly endowed with ingenuity, originality, inspiration, insight, inventiveness, and imagination. In fact, we wouldn't have so many words for it if creativity weren't a universal quality everyone shares.

The creative intelligence portion of this program you begin today will help you release this long-suppressed aspect of your hidden genius.

THE SIX POWERS OF YOUR CREATIVE GENIUS

Unlock your idea smarts and an endless fountain of ideas and inspirations will begin flowing. When you are "off the edge of the map" in life, with no compass to guide you, your creative intelligence will pull you through. Your ingenuity will never run dry, and you will always be able to come up with that fresh idea for the school lunch menu or the eleventh-hour "lightning flash" of inspiration that saves your company from a financial dip following a disastrous marketing plan.

You will be able to

- Summon "instant inspiration" on demand
- Find a way to get things back on track whenever they go wrong

- Stay ahead of competitors with fresh, innovative methods that win you clients others only dream of

- Jump-start creative thinking—even in the midst of the deepest blocks

- Sort inspiration from idiocy—eliminating the duds that won't work, before they go wrong

- Solve any problem by programming your brain's "unconscious idea processor"

LEARN THIS AND YOU'LL NEVER BE STOPPED BY ANYTHING AGAIN

Irma was a dental office manager with twenty years' experience. After the dentist she worked for retired, Irma counted herself lucky to land a new job in the same position for a new dental partnership that had opened only a mile from her home.

But right away, Irma began to run into trouble. "Everything's so different at my new office. They are very up-to-date. They are totally computerized. We had one computer at Dr. Pierce's. They have so many new procedures. Sonic cleansing for the teeth. Implants. Laser drills. An internet website. It's all so new and different. It throws me just thinking about it. I'm having trouble keeping up, and I'm pretty sure the two partners have noticed."

Irma described herself as "foundering." She worried that she had gotten set in her ways after two decades with an elderly dentist. "I'm frightened I don't have the mental flexibility to make such a radical adjustment," she told me.

Irma had been considering resigning from her current position and looking for a job as office manager someplace "a bit more traditional, where it won't be such a mental strain to keep up." But, as Irma said this, I heard the sadness in her voice at not being good enough to succeed at her job and having to settle for something less demanding. She wanted to know if I thought she should quit her current position or if she should stay where she was until things got better.

I replied that she was more than bright enough to pick up any business routine. In large part Irma's problem was that she was accustomed to feeling on top of things all the time, and at her new job she had to strain hard to keep up, which made her feel less competent than she actually was. Over the long run, I told her, I was sure she would adapt and thrive in her current position.

Irma's problem wasn't lack of mental resiliency, I explained, but letting her mind get in too much of a rut. Although, Irma's concern might have appeared remote from creativity, at heart, it was about nothing else. It had been a while since Irma had cause to flex her creative intelligence's capacity for entertaining the new and novel. As a result, it had stiffened and fallen into easy, habitual ways of thinking and doing things.

I prescribed a course of exercises designed to restore Irma's mental flexibility. (The three most effective of these follow here.) It's not unusual for people to become so "stuck" in daily routines and knee-jerk patterns of behavior that, like Irma, they find it difficult to accommodate themselves to change. But like the Tin Man in the *Wizard of Oz*, who loosened when he was rusted tight, a little squirt of the oil of creativity, a bit of exercise, and your idea smarts are as good as new.

THREE PROVEN STRATEGIES FOR UNLOCKING YOUR CREATIVE IQ

Sameness every day is a death knell to creativity. For more complete usage of your idea smarts, diversity and stimulation are the keys. They will get you unstuck from mental habits and ruts and start your creative intelligence flowing.

The three days focused on creative intelligence will restore your mental flexibility to tip-top shape. To keep it there, I recommend the following set of mental gymnastics.

1. *Do something different every day.* Drive to your office by a different route. Purchase your groceries at a different supermarket. Vary your leisure-time activity. If you like movies, go to a play or a hockey match. If you are an indoor type, go outdoors; if you are an outdoor type, read a book. If you habitually wear a tie, go without. If you are habitually untidy, groom yourself as if for an evening out.

2. *Like what you hate.* Next time you are with someone or in a situation you would normally dislike or be critical of, find something to like about it and something nice to say about it instead. If it is someone unpleasant, try to figure out why she responded they way she did and why she would consider that the correct way to react. If it is a disaster at work, or a low grade on a test, try to locate an upside: that it could have been worse or that there is a lesson to be learned so the same thing won't happen again.

3. *Put yourself in someone else's shoes.* This will increase your mental flexibility and develop your ability to view problems from different points of view. Take a few minutes at lunch or after dinner and imagine that you are someone you know rather well. Try to see things through his eyes, think about things the way he would think about them. Then review your own day or concerns. How would this person see them? What would he do?

PUTTING THE POWER OF INSPIRATION TO WORK FOR YOU

On the next page, you will find a four-step technique for calling down the creative lightning called "inspiration" at will. The exercise for day 13 that follows it gives you the same ability to fashion striking, original ideas that put people such as Warren Buffett, Quincy Jones, George Lucas, Denis Waitley, and Dave Thomas where they are today. The exercise for day 14 offers a powerful method of accessing the creative genius that all too typically lies hidden and unsuspected in your deep unconscious. You won't find any of these exercises difficult or intimidating; as with the rest of this program, all three demand nothing more than that you begin to use more consciously talents and abilities you've been using unconsciously, and without suspecting their power, for years.

DAY 12 ———————————————————————————

EXERCISE: INSTANT INSPIRATION

Have you ever been put on the spot for a creative idea? Or tried everything you could think of to solve a problem, without avail? Have you ever wished desperately for the kind of "bolt from the blue" that brought Edison and Mozart their greatest inspirations?

Do you have a pressing situation that requires that kind of creative illumination right now? If so, look at your watch. Perform today's exercise and you can have that desperately needed "bolt from the blue" within the next hour. This exercise will show you how to use your creative intelligence to literally dream up inspired ideas to order.

It combines discoveries from the emerging new science of "ultradian rhythms" with traditional dream "incubation" techniques so that you can incubate creative ideas while you're awake. Like dream incubation, the instant-inspiration exercise takes advantage of the natural capacity of what consciousness researcher Willis Harman, Ph.D., calls the human mind's ability to act like "an unconscious idea processor."

Nearly all scientists and psychologists accept that the unconscious is the source of our creative inspirations. "It is now well established that the unconscious mind is the wellspring of all human creativity," Harman writes. "As with a computer, the operation is automatic, taking place out of sight of the 'screen' of our surface awareness."

Since we all have an unconscious, it follows that we all possess this source of creative inspirations within us. You have probably experienced it yourself. Almost everyone can recall moments when ideas or insights have burst into their consciousness from somewhere in the unconscious, moments when you grasp the solution to a troublesome situation, suddenly have a new perspective that opens new possibilities, or are struck with an illuminating inspiration.

Today you will learn a four-step method for tapping into this aspect of your creative intelligence and summoning creative illuminations whenever you need them. This fantastic exercise actually unleashes the same mental processes responsible for the flashes of insight that made figures such as Albert Einstein, Ludwig von Beethoven, and Warren Buffett famous. For in life, it seems, the race goes not to the strong—or even to the swift—but to those who seemed blessed by what writer Helen Waddell has described as "the lightning flash" of inspiration.

How could you fail if you had the secret of drawing down the divine fire of creative insight practically at will? Super-size the hidden genius of your idea smarts with this powerful technique for solutions to seemingly insoluble and original insights when nothing else will do. Watch your brain power and creative IQ soar.

HE KNEW THE SECRET OF CREATIVITY ON DEMAND

Webster was a young advertising whiz I once worked with at an agency in New Orleans. Our boss, Mr. Bromberg, would summon all his creative staff in without warning when he was hot on the trail of a new client and would expect us to devise a potential award-winning advertising campaign he could pitch to them later that day.

The rest of us would sit around and strain to dream up something original, inspired, fresh, unlike anything that had ever been done for the product before. Without any preparation, this is no easier than it sounds.

I'm afraid to say that as a result we did more straining than creating. All we'd really accomplish was to toss around a few dozen ideas, most of which would never gel for us. Webster never seemed to do any better than the rest of us. After a fruitless couple of hours of this, we'd all be dismissed back to our offices in defeat.

Then, regular as clockwork, about an hour or so later, the boss would call us back into his office. Webster would be sitting on the couch, and our boss would have a smug expression on his face. "Webster here has done it again," Mr. Bromberg would announce. "He's brought me the winning idea."

With this kind of genius, Webster soon became the boss's fair-haired boy.

Finally, the rest of us couldn't stand it and asked Webster his secret. "I don't have a secret, honestly," he replied. "Those meeting always tire me out. So I just stretch out for a while on the couch in my office afterward, just to relax and cool off my brain, and the next thing you know, the whole campaign just pops into my head fully formed."

We were all pretty young at the time and were disappointed. "Stretching out on a couch. That's nothing, I do that all the time. But it doesn't make me a genius," someone laughed. And we all trooped back to our offices.

In our defense, although we didn't get it, neither did Webster. It wasn't until years later, when I learned about ultradian rhythms, that I understood how close we had been to the secret of creativity on demand.

NOW YOU CAN BE A GENIUS—TWELVE TIMES A DAY

It's no secret that many of the world's most celebrated scientific and artistic achievements came in the form of dreams. You've probably had it happen to you. For Thomas Edison, the idea for the first successful lightbulb came, after dozens of failures, in the midst of one of his legendary naps. Robert Louis Stevenson credited a dream with the inspiration for *Dr. Jekyll and Mr. Hyde*, while Beethoven tells of a canon that came to him while "on my way to Vienna yesterday, sleep overtook me in my carriage." Even Descartes's codification of the scientific method itself (which rejects any ideas based on dreams) was the result, not of careful reasoning, but of a dream. All this has led to extensive research into the relationship between creativity and the dreaming state.

What is less well known (and so less appreciated and studied) is that just as many creative inspirations came while the recipient was wide awake, with both eyes open, but in a reflective turn of mind. You may have had this experience, too. Mozart, for instance, wrote that the ideas for his greatest music seemed to come when he was "traveling in a carriage, after a good meal, or during the night when I cannot sleep . . ." Einstein described in a diary how the basis of his Special Theory of Relativity came to him, as did the groundbreaking insights of many other scientists, when he fell into a reverie "during a lengthy streetcar ride." Kipling said the ideas for his stories most often came when he did "not try to think consciously" but, instead, let his mind "drift, wait, obey." The vision that inspired the Sistine Chapel came to Michelangelo when, disgusted with his first attempts, he white-washed his early work, and went out for a stroll in the country. Kekule, the Flemish physicist who finally penetrated the mystery of how molecules connected to one another, explained that after a heavy dinner he turned his "chair to the fire," relaxed, and "the atoms were gamboling before my eyes . . . long rows . . . all twining and twisting in snakelike motion . . . one of the snakes had seized hold of its own tail and whirled mockingly before my eyes."

As a result of discoveries about "ultradian" rhythms, however, we now know that the kinds of moments that trigger these kinds of "waking inspiration" aren't a once-in-a-lifetime—or even a once-in-a-while—thing. Nor even monthly, weekly, or daily.

They occur at least twelve times throughout the waking part of your day and blend with your deepest dream cycles at night. In essence, the same mechanism that is responsible for bestowing brilliant ideas in our dreams is responsible for bestowing them in these moments of waking reverie, as well.

What's more, the science of ultradian rhythms tells us how to identify the moments during the day when your brain is most likely to produce a creative insight. It has also shown us a simple, four-step method that prepares your mind to take advantage of those moments and set off the lightning flash of inspiration you need.

INSTANT INSPIRATION: THE POWER OF YOUR ULTRADIAN RHYTHMS

Only recently has science begun to study the phenomenon of "waking inspiration." Laboratory research in psychobiology has led to a reassessment of these moments and their relationship to what scientists call your "ultradian" rhythms. Ultradian may sound like an alien species out of *Star Wars*, but it simply means body cycles that are shorter than a day. You probably have heard of the body's "circadian" rhythms, the crucial twenty-four-hour cycle that rules our waking-sleeping cycle. But advances in our understanding of the importance of our ultradian rhythms have occurred only during the past few years.

The most important of these rhythms, and the one that produces our lightning bolts of waking inspiration, according to psychobiology researcher Ernest Rossi, Ph.D., is "the basic 90 to 120 minutes Activity-Recuperation cycle." During the active cycle, the "first hour or so of this rhythm," Rossi writes, "we swing upward on a wave of heightened physical and mental alertness and energy, our skills, memory, and learning ability at their peak for dealing with the world around us." Then, Rossi says, comes the recuperation part of the cycle, when "many of our systems of mind and body attempt to turn inward for a period of heightened healing and recharging."

At this point, Rossi notes, we enter an altered state of consciousness when we feel a sense of well-being and, as a result, the unconscious comes close to the surface—exactly as it does when we dream. It is during this vital "fifteen to twenty minutes" of the recuperation cycle that our waking illuminations come and the potential of programming your mind for instant inspiration begins.

It's easy to tell when the recuperation phase of the ultradian rhythm begins and your unconscious is about to surface. Typical indications include sudden yawning, feeling a need to stretch or move around, sudden craving for a snack, absent-minded jiggling and doodling, and finding yourself staring blankly off into space.

Fifteen or twenty minutes after the recuperation cycle begins, our bodily systems, refreshed, swing back into the active portion of the 90 to 120 minute activity-recuperation ultradian rhythm again.

DRAWING DOWN GENIUS IN FOUR EASY STEPS

Psychologists and dream workers from Henry Reed, Ph.D., to Patricia Garfield, Ph.D., have long recommended the following four-step process for incubating dreams to solve problems and summon creative inspirations. This technique works pretty much the same way clouds are seeded or pearls grown in oysters. An idea is planted in the mind before sleep, where it lodges in your unconscious—much like a command in a computer program—and an answering dream forms around it.

The four steps for unlocking your hidden genius through dream incubation are:

1. For a few minutes after going to bed, focus your attention on the problem with the intention of solving it.

2. Go to sleep.

3. Dream the solution; on either the first night, or within the first few, you should dream a viable solution.

4. Write down your dream solution and then give it a real-life test.

What do these steps have to do with ultradian rhythms? Just this: You no longer have to wait until you go to bed at night and dream to take advantage of this process and incubate a creative inspiration. Because the same mechanism is responsible for both the deep-dreaming (rapid eye movement) cycle and the ultradian-recuperation rhythm, you can program your "unconscious idea processor" to produce inspirations for you during any of the twelve daytime ultradian cycles.

CREATIVE INTELLIGENCE BUILDER: INSTANT INSPIRATION

This is a nonpareil lazy person's exercise. The only thing you need is a problem that needs to be solved or a situation that calls for an ounce of inspiration. All you contribute is about two minutes of thought. After that, you stretch out, relax, and your unconscious does the rest of the work.

The next time you are in need of a creative illumination, wait until the start of the recuperation phase of your next ultradian cycle. Watch for indications such as yawning, staring abstractedly at nothing, or any of the other signs mentioned previously. You won't have to wait long. (Remember, you have one every 90 to 120 minutes.)

Then

1. Just before or while entering your next ultradian-recuperation cycle, focus your attention for a few moments on reviewing the major elements, the major problems, what you ultimately need to accomplish, and your resolve to solve it.

2. Let go of the issue consciously, turning your attention elsewhere and allowing the problem to simmer around in your unconscious. Then stretch out in your chair, or on a couch, while your body draws itself inward, shifting to your unconscious.

3. Allow your reverie to proffer the solution. The result is always an answering illumination, which flashes from your unconscious at some unexpected moment, typically while you are musing about something else (Aunt Monica's birthday, for instance). (If the inspiration you are seeking fails to come during your first ultradian cycle, repeat steps 1-3 during each of the following cycles. In most instances, you should receive an insight before the end of the day.)

4. Put your inspiration into practice to see how well it works. (While in most cases the first illumination is right, not every inspiration is a valid one.)

It's important to note that only step 1 requires any action or effort on your part. Steps 2 and 3 are automatic, given step 1. Your ultradian cycle and your unconscious will take care of the rest and the result will be the illumination you need. Following up on that insight is, of course, up to you.

THE POWER TECHNIQUE YOU'LL LEARN TOMORROW

You won't always have time to wait to hitchhike on your next ultradian cycle for an inspiration. The exercise for day 13 shows you how you can craft original, profitable ideas with only two minutes of prior thought. The exercise will do the rest.

DAY 13 ————————————————————————
EXERCISE: REVERSAL

You can't always hope to take advantage of your ultradian rhythms for creative inspiration. Sometimes you simply aren't in a position to wait fifteen minutes or half an hour until the start of the next recuperation phase. Other times, you may be working with a team against a deadline. Or, you may have been mandated to present a variety of options and ideas.

Today's creative intelligence exercise is another of those brain-friendly approaches to unlocking your hidden genius. Can you name the opposites of "hot," "good," and "tall"? If your responses were "cold," "bad," and "short," then you'll have no difficulty using this technique to coin arresting, original ideas in minutes.

Originality is the essential difference between those who go all the way to the top and the rest of us. While others flail away blindly with their heads against a wall with the same failed approaches, there are no limits for someone who can find an original way, under, around, through, or over. Whether you are working with the public, managing a department, shepherding your company through the rocky waters of today's business climate, hoping to be the next best-selling hip-hop group, or aiming for early retirement, originality is the grease that makes the going easy.

You can use today's technique to tap your creative genius any time you are in urgent need of a fresh idea, or when you're simply drawing a blank over a long-standing problem. It's also an ideal method of jump-starting your creative juices when they aren't flowing as well as you like, or when they are stubbornly refusing to flow at all.

YOU HAVE IT—AND IT'S WORTH ONE MILLION DOLLARS

It's not unusual to get stuck for ideas. It kind of goes with the territory of being human. You might consider this tendency the downside of being able to learn. Here's how we become blocked in our efforts to create fresh, original notions.

During childhood, when our minds are learning for the first time about the world around us, each day is a constant succession of new and unfamiliar situations, discoveries, reactions, and assumptions. By our twenties, however, most of the basic situations in life have become all too familiar—angry bosses, being short of cash, rejection in love, someone swerving into our lane on the freeway—and we have developed an established set of responses to them. Familiar responses are terrific for dealing with familiar situations, most of the time, allowing us to respond quickly, without wasting time and energy reasoning out how we should react.

But they have disadvantages, too. For instance, we can come to rely on familiar responses and assumptions to carry us through situations, and we have a hard time deciding how to respond to something that's without precedent in our lives. Worse, we tend to become blind to any outcome that does not fit in with our normal perceptions and assumptions.

When the Aztecs, who had never seen horses and did not ride animals, first sighted Spanish soldiers riding horseback, their previous assumptions initially kept them from seeing that it was a man mounted on an animal. Instead, they saw what they described as "a strange animal with two heads, two arms, and four legs." The Aztecs' prior experiences had made it possible for them to assume there could be previously unknown animals (presumably because they encountered new species from time to time), but not that human beings would ride one.

Indigenous peoples aren't the only ones limited by familiar responses and assumptions. The history of the technological age is replete with just as many examples. Though blinking lights had been around for more than five decades, it wasn't until the 1940s that anyone thought of putting them on the back of cars. Until then everyone just went along with the familiar response from horse and buggy days of indicating a turn with hand signals, or in imitation of them, by pulling the lever on a driver's side mechanical arm that pointed straight out for left or straight up for right.

The age of computers is just as guilty of this kind of blind, unthinking response in the face of change. The first computers in the early fifties were operated by typing in long sequences of command numbers and letters, and computer experts and designers got used to its being that way. So when it came time to design the home PC, they fell back on the familiar way of operating it—typing in long commands. The result was the near failure of the home PC. It was only when Steve Jobs broke away from the familiar responses and assumptions that he realized the PC could be made to type its own commands; all the user should have to do is click a cute little icon to initiate the process.

As you can see, original ideas are so fundamental to success you can't afford the lack of them to stand in your way for very long. Luckily, there's a blindingly simple process for overcoming the limiting, but familiar assumptions that prevent you from scheming up fresh, original notions. I call this technique "reversal," and it draws on a mental skill you use every day.

"Reversal" gives you the same ability that has enabled tens of thousands of people to become millionaires. (This is another of those claims I know you will find difficult to believe. But suspend your disbelief until the end of the chapter, and you will discover every word is true.)

REVERSAL: YOUR PATH TO PURE ORIGINALITY

I used to recommend reversal to my fiction-writing students, without understanding its wider application to problem solving and getting a person out of a creative dead end. I told them that when they drew a blank while writing a scene, or found themselves writing a scene that began to feel dull or clichéd, they could always spice things up and find a fresh approach if they simply turned the situation inside out and reversed it. Say you have to write a scene where two characters reveal their love for each other, I'd tell my prospective authors. There have been millions of versions of this scene, and it's hard to think of a fresh approach to it. But reverse that scene, stand it on its head, have the two characters in love, but they think they hate each other, have them argue furiously, as Lerner and Loewe do in the famous "I Hate You Henry Higgins" scene in *My Fair Lady*, and you have a scene that holds audiences spellbound, wondering how it will turn out.

Another great example of this, given by director Vincente Minnelli in his autobiography was his handling of *The Clock*, the story of a young soldier (Robert Walker) on a twenty-four-hour leave who is about to embark for the war and the young girl (Judy Garland) he falls in love with, filmed against a real-life deadline with Walker himself scheduled to leave for the war—and no time for rewrites. Stuck with the project at the last minute, Minnelli found the script one long series of clichés: the cute little kid they see in the park who makes the boy and girl reflect on having children of their own and the friendly cabdriver who takes them home, where they meet the loving couple emblematic of the joys of marital old age. With rewrites ruled out, Minnelli decided to reverse every cliché: the cute kid became a terror who kicks our hero, but "the kind of terror you want your kid to be," and the old couple do nothing but argue and bicker throughout their scene, only here and there revealing with a facial expression the true bond of affection that still unites them even after all these years. (*The Clock*, needless to say, was a popular and critical hit, lauded for its warm irony.)

Here are a few more of my favorite examples from the world of literature and the media you are probably familiar with. Everyone knew readers wanted a long historical romance to have a happy ending, until Margaret Mitchell reversed that and wrote *Gone with the Wind*, and it became an international bestseller. Everyone knew television series had to be about something—a crusty old man who suddenly finds himself the guardian of three young orphans or a dedicated band of cops fighting crime—until Jerry Seinfeld reversed that, and *Seinfeld*, a show about nothing, became a hit. Nineteenth-century readers knew vampires were deformed, cadaver-like creatures, with bloodless faces and protruding fangs, until Bram Stoker reversed that, and *Dracula*, the suave vampire and one of the best-selling books of the past hundred years, was given life. Everyone knew private eyes had to be two-fisted he-men until Agatha Christie invented Hercule Poirot, and Rex Stout set pen to Nero Wolfe, two of the most enduring characters in detective literature.

HOW YOU CAN STRIKE CREATIVE PAYDIRT WITH REVERSAL—EVERY TIME

The goal of today's exercise is to free you from the limitations of familiar assumptions so your creative intelligence can come into play. A great way to do this when you are at a loss for a new idea or solution is simply to take one's bedrock assumptions and *reverse* them. As with other super brain power techniques, this may sound simple in principle, but don't be fooled, the results will seem to be far out of proportion to the effort.

In fact, fortunes in professions far outside the arts or sciences—in construction, real estate, pharmaceuticals, computers, the food-service industry, and a thousand other businesses—have been founded on ideas that consisted of nothing more than a normal, everyday assumption someone turned upside-down and backward.

A retired southerner named Harlan Sanders took the idea that restaurants should offer a varied fare so as to have something for everyone and reversed it. The result: Col. Sanders Kentucky Fried Chicken, a restaurant that served only a single entree. Families used to go to theaters (and hush children constantly) to see motion pictures, until television made it easier to stay home for entertainment. "Boys should be boys" and "girls should be girls" was a traditional response, until Little Richard, David Bowie, Jim Baily, Ru Paul and other performers reversed that assumption, resulting in international fame and celebrity. Everybody goes to bookstores for books. Amazon.com reversed that assumption. The result: People began shopping virtual bookstores, their purchases delivered by mail. Retail industry wisdom was that to make a profit with a chain store, it must be located in an urban or suburban area with a dense population near a major traffic artery. Sam Walton stood that assumption on its crown, and Wal-Mart, the result, was the world's most profitable discount chain, with operations thriving in smaller communities starved for low-cost shopping.

Examples could go on and on. Likely you are familiar with a few yourself, or you have even used reversal without being aware that that was the principle involved. The point is that when one does pause to reflect, the true power of reversal—to overthrow our familiar ways of thinking and point the way toward original ideas and approaches—stands revealed.

CREATIVE INTELLIGENCE BUILDER: REVERSAL

The reversal exercise is remarkably simple. It takes only a couple of minutes of thought, and it will kick-start your creative IQ. It takes your basic assumptions about a problem, helps you formulate them in "is" statements, and then (using a form of mental jujitsu to reverse them), creates a series of striking, original ideas. (As examples, I am going to show how the basic principles of reversal lay behind three world-famous food-service fortunes.)

You will need a pen and a sheet of paper at first. But once you have learned the technique, you will be able to do it easily in your head.

1. *List your basic assumptions about your problem*, or whatever you need a creative nudge with, as a series of "is" statements that describe how something "is" or how it "is" related to something else. This will help you focus your assumptions by putting them into clear, declarative statements. (If you were an entrepreneur with a yen to be a restaurateur and you were looking for an original concept that would stand out from the competition, you might write your assumptions as: "A restaurant is an establishment where people come to eat food." "A restaurant is an establishment where people pay for the food they eat." "A restaurant is an establishment where people can find varied fare to please any palate.")

2. *Beginning with what you consider your most important assumption*, write a sentence reversing each assumption to create its opposite. This is another reason for using "is" sentences. It makes turning them back on themselves easier. (Take our first restaurant assumption; Thomas Monaghan, founder of Domino's Pizza, might have reversed that by writing, "A restaurant is an establishment that sends food out to people." Or take the second assumption: Earl Clifton, founder of Los Angeles's legendary Clifton's Cafeterias chain, might have reversed it by writing, "A restaurant is an establishment that gives food away." That's what he did in the 1930s, serving millions of bowls of a free, if slightly flavorless soup stock fortified with every essential vitamin, protein, and mineral. Defying the odds, the act brought him appreciative paying patrons, Clifton prospered where many failed, and the chain lasted well into the 1970s. As for the third assumption, Col. Sanders might have reversed it by writing, "A restaurant is an establishment that has a limited menu, focused on a single entree.")

3. *Review each of your reversed assumptions.* Ask yourself, is there evidence that supports or contradicts it? (Thomas Monaghan might have noted that people were often willing to drive several miles for take-out Chinese food and pizza on Friday and Saturday nights; that might support the notion of a restaurant that delivers its food to the customers. Earl Clifton might have said that goodwill and word of mouth are the two main ways restaurants build their customer base, and giving the poor thousands of bowls of nutritious soup that costs me only pennies could be the ideal way to generate both. Col. Sanders might have observed that pizza and barbecue restaurants were becoming very popular in the post-World War II era and that an establishment specializing in the kind of old-fashioned, finger-licking fried chicken grandmother used to make just might attract a clientele, too.)

4. *Try out any of your reversed assumptions that seem as if they might have validity.*

THE POWER TECHNIQUE YOU'LL LEARN TOMORROW

Day 14 will present one of the most powerful strategies for brainstorming creative ideas ever offered. It super-sizes your brain power by wedding the body's natural biological rhythms to a potent dream incubation, to produce lightning flashes of inspiration literally "out of the blue."

DAY 14 ————————————————————————————————————
EXERCISE: SUPER BRAINSTORMING

Whether you are under pressure from your competition to improve the quality of your product or seek a way to convince that touchy coworker in the adjoining office to cool his smoking without setting off a "battle royale," or whether you work in an innovative business such as toys, the arts, marketing, and the like, genuine creativity is a quality in short supply. Creativity can't be counterfeited or imitated—or it's not creativity. But there are occasions when it's oh, so necessary.

Sometimes, for example, when you solve a problem, you can find yourself facing another one that only a dash of original thinking can solve. You might unblock a bottleneck in production only to discover a shortage of parts the slowdown concealed. Other times, you try everything logic and past experience can suggest and still remain stymied. Or you go through all the techniques in a dozen books on conciliation and positive communication, and still can't get through to your coworker. Whatever the solution is, it will clearly take something different, creative.

There's a scene in almost every comedy where someone puts his or her coins in a soft-drink machine, waits a long time, the machine fails to dispense the drink, and the person walk away disgusted, giving the machine an angry kick on leaving—and, of course, the kick causes the soda can, which has been jammed up somewhere in the mechanism, to fall in the slot, just as the hapless one has walked out of sight.

Occasionally, your brain gets jammed the same way. When that occurs, you can't think of a thing. And what you do think of isn't very creative. You are in the midst of a mental and creative logjam, dry of ideas and out of inspiration.

Your brain, however, doesn't need to remain jammed. You can get it unstuck with the mental equivalent of a good old-fashioned kick. Most techniques for giving your creative IQ a good, healthy kick involve some aspect of "brainstorming" ideas. Today's exercise is called "super brainstorming" because it takes all the effort out of brainstorming by giving your idea smarts a quick jolt, the same way doctors shoot a quick jolt of electricity into a stopped heart to get it started. And all you need to do is fill out a few 3 × 5 cards. Could unlocking your hidden genius be easier?

HOW CREATIVITY CAN BE AS SIMPLE AS ONE, TWO, THREE . . .

Often we draw a blank in our search for inspiration, coming up with all the wrong ideas, or with none at all. We fail, in short, to arrive at an acceptable mental destination. When this happens, one of the best ways to get your idea smarts churning is to break a problem down into its basic attributes and then tantalize your hidden genius with novel, provocative, even nonsensical combinations of those attributes. (This is a lot like working up your creative appetite with mental *hors d'oeuvres.*) This will stimulate your creative intelligence, set you thinking, and result a number of valid, ingenious ideas.

One way to mix up attributes such as this is to create what appear to be outrageous, extravagant metaphors comparing the elements of your problem to some randomly chosen object. Business consultant Robert W. Olson, in *The Art of Creative Thinking*, describes how this process could be used to yield original insights about organizational structure. Picking the lowly matchbox as something about as remote from the structure of corporations as possible, he generates the following thought-provoking comparisons.

The matchbox: Striking surface on two sides

Organizational metaphor: The protection an organization needs against strikes

The matchbox: Six sides

Organizational metaphor: Six essential organizational divisions

The matchbox: Sliding center section

Organizational metaphor: Heart of organization should be mobile or flexible

The matchbox: Made of cardboard

Organizational metaphor: Inexpensive, disposable method of operation and structure

That's proof positive of the profound, creative insights using this kind of tantalizing, even absurd random juxtaposition of attributes can produce. Today's exercise, a variant of a technique first cooked up in the laboratories of creativity researchers, formalizes this process and makes it automatic. You use 3 × 5 cards to create random, thought-provoking combinations of attributes. It takes all the worry out of coming up with novel mental mixtures and makes creativity as easy as one . . . , two . . . , three.

The intent is to stimulate your creative IQ, hot-wire it, and get the mental electricity moving by shaking up your normal way of see-ing things. If the essence of creativity is devising original combinations of ideas to solve everyday problems, then the super-brainstorming technique is one of the simplest ways to devise original combinations of ideas.

SIX STEPS TO A CORNUCOPIA OF CREATIVE IDEAS

The super-brainstorming technique has a zero failure rate. Its six steps are warranted to start a cornucopia of creative thoughts, ideas, images, solutions, speculations, suppositions, combinations, inspira-tions, and answers pouring through your mind. The only effort you make is to write down a few attributes, along with how they might be changed, and then shuffle the cards. These six steps are:

1. *List the key attributes or categories you have to work with.* Think of as many as you can. The more categories you generate now, the more original ideas you can generate later.

2. *Starting with the first attribute or category, write ten ideas for how it might be handled, each on its own 3 × 5 card.* It doesn't matter how realistic or how wild your inspirations are, write down everything that occurs to you. Sometimes the wack-iest ideas turn out to have a hidden value.

3. *Repeat with each of the other attributes or categories, using a different colored marker or card for each and piling each category in its own stack facedown before you.* Don't hurry the process, you might miss a critical inspiration.

4. *Turn over the top card on each stack (attribute/category), try to dream up a way of linking the ideas for each to solve your problem, however farfetched it might be, and write it down.* Do your best to think of an idea that might link your disparate elements together to and make something out of them.

5. *Repeat this process until you have ten completely different ideas written down and have turned over the last card in each stack.* No matter how wild the combinations of ideas you get, even if you strike upon what you feel is the ideal combination right away, don't stop until you have worked all ten cards in each category, listing every combination the cards produce.

6. *If you haven't arrived at a solution, shuffle each stack separately, place them facedown, and repeat steps 4 and 5.* This will produce new combinations. By teasing your brain with different mixtures of attributes such as this, you will eventually jog it into producing a useful inspiration.

There's no rule that says you have to base your answers on any single run-through of the cards, or even on an actual combination you draw. They might spark some other, but germane idea altogether. Mix and match attributes in any way that seems to make sense or to work for you. The point of this exercise is to use the power of randomness to jog your mind into a creative brainstorm.

CREATIVE INTELLIGENCE BUILDER: POWER BRAINSTORMING

To do this exercise, you'll need a deck of 3 × 5 cards and a pen. For greater visual clarity, I suggest a whole set of markers of many different colors. Then:

1. *List on a sheet of paper the key elements or categories you have to work with.* (Once a furniture manufacturer asked my friend Gina, a children's artist, to design a chair for children. Her categories were "materials," "legs," "arms," "color," "comfort," "seat," "back," "children's themes.")

2. *Starting with the first category, write ten ideas for it, each on its own 3 × 5 card.* (Beginning with "materials," Gina wrote a card each for every possible substance that occurred to her, wacky or not, including "wood," "plastic," "steel," "foam," "concrete," "mushroom," "marshmallow," "chocolate," "feathers," "balloons.")

3. *Do the same with all the other categories, using a different colored marker or card for each category, and piling each category in its own stack.* (For the category of "legs," Gina wrote cards for "tri-cornered," "four-legged," "six-legged," "pedestal," "cube," "stool" (like mushroom), "pyramid." For the category of "color," she wrote "primary colors," "pastel," "rainbow-striped," "polka-dots." For "children's themes," she made cards listing such perennials as "cotton candy," "marshmallows," "elephants," "dinosaurs," "spaceships." She also filled out cards for the other categories she had listed, placing the cards for each in a separate stack.)

4. *Turn over the top card on each stack (category), try to dream up a way of linking the ideas for each category to solve your problem,* however farfetched it might be, and write it down. (Gina's top cards were: in materials, "metal," in color, "pastel," and in theme, "marshmallow." Gina's fertile mind conjured the image of a pastel, marshmallow-shaped chair made out of metal.)

5. *Repeat the process until you have ten completely different ideas written down and have turned over the last card in each stack.* (On first thought, the idea of a pastel, marshmallow-shaped foam chair might seem as if it would be ideal. But, Gina would have to continue working through all the cards, anyway.)

6. *If you haven't arrived at a solution, shuffle each stack separately, place them facedown, and repeat steps 4 and 5.* (In Gina's case, her ultimate design for the chair incorporated many elements

from the first set of cards, with some additions borrowed from later combinations. The result was a best-selling set of soft, plastic beanbag chairs in the shape of pastel-colored marshmallows.)

By teasing your brain this way with different combinations, you will ultimately jog it into producing a useful inspiration.

FOUR WAYS PEOPLE HAVE USED SUPER BRAINSTORMING TO HELP THEM TOWARD SUCCESS

When Jamal found the company he owned was producing an unaccountable number of defective microchips, he applied the super-brainstorming technique to quality improvement and identified a number of ways he could alter for the better key steps. Doreen, who operated a small New Age bookstore, found super brainstorming helped her design a striking window display for the new Leslie Feinberg book. Amina found it helped her devise novel sales approaches to overcoming prospects' objections to the executive-search program she represented. Jorge found it helped him dream up attention-getting menus and promotional campaigns for his barbecue restaurant.

THE POWER TECHNIQUE YOU WILL LEARN TOMORROW

Beginning with day 15, you will release the unsuspected power of your physical intelligence. This is truly such an underappreciated capacity of human beings that each of these three exercises could multiply your brain power by 100 percent. Tomorrow, you will super-size your brain power with the awesome ability of your body smarts to warn you of potential danger and guide you toward important opportunities. On day 16, you will discover the secret of learning any job the first time, every time. On day 17, you will acquire the knack of using your physical intelligence to create instant rapport and approval with anyone you meet.

The Fifth Key—

UNLOCKING YOUR PHYSICAL GENIUS

WHAT'S YOUR PHYSICAL IQ?

This quiz rates physical intelligence. Don't let an initial low score intimidate you. Whatever your score, you can further develop and refine your body smarts by completing the three exercises that follow.

To find your physical IQ, check any phrases that apply. Do you

☐ Learn fastest when you can get your hands on a tool or machine and do it yourself, rather than listening to someone point out what to do, watching an instructional video or reading a manual?

☐ Belong to a gym and maintain a regular routine of weekly visits?

☐ Frequently have, and act on "gut" instincts—actual pains or warm glows in your abdomen—that have guided you toward productive decisions and away from less desirable outcomes?

☐ Have a talent for mimicking the way other people move and speak?

☐ Become restless if you have to sit or stand or work in one position, or at one repetitive task for any length of time?

☐ Work in a profession that has a physical aspect—surgeon, carpenter, typist, file clerk, hardware engineer?

☐ Enjoy working with your hands at gardening, household repairs, building a backyard barbecue?

☐ Have a subscription to ESPN or some other cable sports channels and are you more likely to watch championship figure skating, Olympic gymnastics, or a local ball game than watch talk shows or prime-time dramas?

175

❏ Get your best ideas during walks, jogging, doing the dishes, painting the house, or raking the lawn?

❏ Talk with your hands and move excitedly when communicating with others?

❏ Enjoy slapstick comedy such as Laurel and Hardy or the Police Academy movies, or like to play physical pranks on friends?

❏ Frequently head off into the "great outdoors" for the weekend?

❏ Have symptoms of hyperactivity?

❏ Spend your weekends in athletic pursuits, devoting your time off to tennis, golf, or prepping for a marathon?

❏ Shine in any physical activity, such as track, swimming, or football?

❏ Possess physical grace and coordination?

Scoring: Add up the number of boxes you checked.

If your score was between 1 and 4, your body smarts remain largely undeveloped. If we were talking about physical muscles rather than mental muscles, you would be the proverbial "ninety-eight-pound weakling." However, the three days of exercises you are about to begin will start you on your way toward the body smarts of a Jackie Chan or a Michelle Kwan.

If your score was between 5 and 8, your physical intelligence is still in need of the strong boost you will get from this section of the program.

If your score was between 9 and 13, you are above average in body smarts. A bit more effort, however, would catapult you to the top of the class in physical IQ.

If your score was between 14 and 16, your body smarts are as high as high can be. If you aren't a journalist, ad whiz, minister, sales person, or earning your living from your physical intelligence, you are letting valuable talents go to waste. You probably don't need these exercises, but you will probably want to do them just for the fun of it.

UNLOCKING YOUR
PHYSICAL INTELLIGENCE

This last week of the program will put you in direct touch with your innate body smarts. Physical intelligence is ignored in virtually all mental-training programs. But in real life, you can't ignore it—your body plays a central role in everything you do.

Almost all of the activities and tasks that we engage in every day have a physical component. That's true whether we're marking student tests, delivering pizza, demonstrating a printer to a potential customer, installing wiring, writing a report, managing an office, washing the car, buying a new pair of jeans at the mall, driving to and from work, hiking, playing badminton, cooking, or e-mailing requests to rich donors for contributions to the church renovation fund. Even our best ideas can take the form of a "gut" feeling, such as when our love for another spreads warmth through the chest, or when some unconscious fear creates a sinking sensation in the belly.

There's no point in educating the brain unless you educate the body's brain. Mental peak performance means nothing if your body's performance is only a fraction of its potential. Often, you have more to gain by exercising your physical intelligence than by exercising your physique.

Day 15 will put you in touch with your body's intelligence in a manner you never dreamed possible. Day 16 gives a strategy that enables anyone to increase performance and master physical skills in record time (even if you have found this kind of learning difficult in the past). Day 17 presents the capstone exercise, which will give you the kind of body smarts that allows great speakers and sales wizards to win the confidence and agreement of others.

Even if you consider yourself the possessor of a well-developed physical IQ, you will discover these exercises have a unique twist that challenges it in a whole new way. But there's a big difference between exercising your body and exercising your body smarts. Or, if you're someone who rates your body smarts low, and you tend to see yourself as awkward, clumsy, and uncoordinated, these three days will provide you with a revolutionary new view of the role your body can play in propelling you to success. (If you're not certain about where you rank in terms of verbal intelligence, the What's Your Physical IQ quiz on page 175 will help you rate it.)

A SIMPLE TECHNIQUE THAT BOOSTED A WOMAN'S PRODUCTIVITY

Martha had been downsized during a merger from her position as secretary at a large publishing firm. After several months of searching, she finally found employment in the mailroom of a small publisher specializing in 12-step recovery-themed books. The stockroom would bring her the orders; Martha had to double-check the invoice against the actual books she received, estimate by eye the amount of plastic "bubble" wrap the order would take, pull out the wrap, cut it, nestle the books in it, fold the wrap, tape it shut at the top and both ends, pick the right sized envelope, slip in the order, seal the envelope, strip the mailing label from the invoice, paste it on, and then put the entire package in a cart for UPS delivery.

It was time-consuming, high-volume work and it made high demands on Martha's physical coordination and productivity. Martha was in her third week on the job—and just didn't seem able to keep up with the work the way previous mailroom employees had. She felt clumsy, awkward, and could never find an efficient rhythm where it all came together and she could do things effortlessly. Then, at one of my seminars, as I was presenting the idea of physical intelligence, Martha raised her hand and challenged me for a way she could make practical use of it the next morning at work to solve her problem.

Martha's specific problem was getting the swing of the packaging process so she could sail along at the speed she needed to keep up with her job's demands. The technique I suggested has been used successfully to improve performance at almost every kind of physical skill. It doesn't matter if your personal challenge is typing, operating machinery, preparing a banquet, paperwork, presenting yearly earnings reports to a board of directors within the tightly allotted time, electronic video editing, bricklaying, making sandwiches, tennis, golf, baseball, or quilting. (I am even informed that it has been applied beneficially during lovemaking.)

I didn't hear from Martha again for over a year. She had retained the mailroom position and was now attending business college in the evenings. The technique I had given her during the workshop had saved her job, she told me. But that is not the point.

The point is you—and *your* body smarts. The point is what you can do with your physical intelligence once it has been unlocked by the strategies such as the one I taught Martha and the others that night. (If you'd like to benefit from it, too, it's number two under "Three Proven Strategies for Unlocking Your Physical IQ" on page 182.)

YOUR BODY: SMARTER THAN YOU THINK— SMARTER THAN YOU *CAN* THINK

You accidentally knock a glass of water off your office desk. Without an instant's thought, your hand darts down and intercepts the goblet before it can shatter against the floor.

Your company hires a new employee to work with your department. Despite a favorable first impression, you get a knot in your stomach every time this person is around. Later, the new employee turns out to be the kind who spends all her time gossiping and spreading rumors.

After months of practicing and consciously thinking about the intricacies of that new tennis stroke—and failing miserably—you find yourself in midgame, rising effortlessly to meet an almost impossible shot and following through perfectly for the score that wins the game.

Your contracting company has been hired to pour cement for a new construction site. When you first see the site, it "feels" as if the job should take about six and a half hours to mix and pour. The next day, when you are finished and the last bag has been mixed, you glance at a clock and discover it took exactly six and a half hours.

Normally, we tend to think of "physical" and "intelligence" as almost opposites—antithetical qualities that, like oil and water, do not readily mix. Athletes are typically not pictured as intellectual heavyweights; and we generally do not picture highly brainy people as physically imposing and adept. That's why to most people the idea of "physical intelligence" sounds like an oxymoron.

But, as the preceding examples prove, there are times when your body is far smarter and quicker than you are, than you can be. The body, too, has its own memory, decision-making circuits, and wisdom. This view is supported by research at San Francisco's Mount Zion Hospital. Psychologists there wanted to know whether, when we are performing at our optimum, the body is being controlled by the conscious mind or by some separate subsystem of the brain.

Their research showed that while it takes about *four tenths of a second* for the conscious mind to register a new perception, whether it's the touch of a raindrop or a sound from the radio, in emergencies such as dropping a glass, or a fall down the stairs, or the sight of a puck shooting toward your position in a hockey game, your body can take in the situation, calculate the precise movement and speed needed to save it, and respond—all in less than *one tenth of a second.* That's *three tenths of a second faster* than your conscious mind can respond. Could even the most sophisticated computer meet such a challenge?

Much the same could be said about the complexities involved in your body's "knowing" there was something off-kilter about that new employee when everything you were aware of added up in her favor. Or how you could estimate so precisely the time it would take to complete a physical activity such as pouring cement. Or the times your body suddenly rose to a challenge in the middle of a game and performed flawlessly. In every case, the act was almost effortless, your body responding from some intrinsic knowledge of its own.

As human-potential guru Michael Murphy writes in *The Future of the Body*, a wealth of scientific research verifies the almost superhuman abilities our bodies sometimes possess. "Data from many fields," he notes, "—including medicine, anthropology, sports, psychical research, and comparative religious studies—[prove the existence of] extraordinary versions of most, if not all, of our basic attributes, among them sensorimotor, kinesthetic [and other] bodily processes. The evidence suggests that we harbor a range of extraordinary physical capacities."

THE POWER OF PHYSICAL INTELLIGENCE

It's easy to see how these findings could hold profound implications for athletes and gymnasts and for others, such as actors, laborers, and musicians, whose work also involves a large physical component. But it isn't as easy to see how they relate to people in business, academia, and other professions that seem to draw more on the mind than on the body.

But take the computer as an example. More and more of us are spending more and more time working with computers. But we seldom consider just how much physical activity this incurs. Intently manipulating a mouse or working at a keyboard may not seem strenuous. But, just ask a secretary who has to do data entry all day and you will hear a different story. Or talk to anyone who suffers from carpal-tunnel syndrome. (The novelist and amateur boxer Norman Mailer once said that working for eight hours at a typewriter was just as grueling as eight rounds in a boxing ring.) And, all this is true of just about any office task.

SEVEN POWERS YOU GAIN WHEN YOU SUPER-SIZE YOUR BODY SMARTS

If you want to "do it better" in the boardroom, the bedroom, or the playing field, you need a high physical IQ. Body smarts contribute to your overall intelligence quotient in many ways. Work your way through the exercises for these three days, and you will have

- Greater physical coordination—perform any physical activity better

- The ability to pick the right course in any situation by tapping in on your "gut feelings" and other forms of your body wisdom

- Increased productivity and efficiency, without increased effort

- A talent for "speed-learning" physical skills, with almost zero mistakes

- The stamina to work longer, absorb greater stress, and resist illness better than others

- An ability to achieve mastery by turning any task over to the body and letting it "do the walking"

- The know-how to use "body language" to gain the confidence and cooperation of others

You can see what a plus all of these skills would be. And those are just a few of the amazing benefits you'll enjoy when you super-size your bodily intelligence.

THREE PROVEN STRATEGIES FOR UNLOCKING YOUR PHYSICAL IQ

As you grow in body smarts over the next weeks and months, give the proven strategies a try anytime you feel the need of an additional boost.

1. *Get used to your body in new ways.* This helps keep your physical intelligence honed and at its peak. If you are right-handed, do everything with your left hand for the next few hours (and vice-versa if you are left-handed). At some point during the day, use your feet to pick up something, or to open and close a door. Read a page in a book held upside down. Eat your dinner with chopsticks instead of a spoon and fork (or vice-versa if you more typically eat your dinner with chopsticks).

2. *Time your breathing with whatever action you are performing.* One excellent strategy for achieving a natural rhythm in your work is to allow your breathing to coincide with your efforts. The breath has an in-and-out twofold rhythm. And when you think about it, so do most actions—from striking a key or cutting a pipe or slicing carrots, to the back and then forward swing of baseball, tennis, and golf. Repeat this rhythm. If it's golf, breathe in on your backswing and exhale with your downstroke. Tim Galloway, one of many peak performance coaches who uses this method for educating the body's brain, notes that for best results you should "match your strokes with your breathing, not your breathing with your strokes. You will find that in a short period any jerkiness and irregularity of rhythm will begin to fade away."

3. *Comedians, singers, politicians, and others whose livelihood depends on how people react to them, draw on their physical intel-*

ligence and heighten the impact they make by using body language. Research reveals that how we respond to a speaker is determined as much by body language as by the actual content of what he or she is saying. You can increase the effect your body language has on other people and become more conscious of how the body language of others affects you by watching "reality-based" television shows. Next time you're watching the news, notice the different body languages the anchor uses while reporting on positive, upbeat stories and on negative, downbeat ones. On game shows, zero in on the telltale signs that reveal nervousness or confidence. On Judge Judy or some other courtroom show, observe how people react when telling the truth and when they are caught in a lie. Could you tell beforehand that the person was lying? What gave it away? Apply these lessons to your own body language. When trying to convince someone of something (say your boss into giving you a raise, or a prospect you hope will become a sale) review your body language; it won't help your case if you are inadvertently using the same posture or intonation reporters use when they are conveying bad news. In general, when interacting with others, avoid postures associated with nervousness and lack of truthfulness. Cultivate those that project confidence and honesty.

PUTTING THE POWER OF THE BODY TO WORK FOR YOU

As with the rest of the super brain power program, developing your physical intelligence doesn't call for special abilities or effort. You won't be called on for the kind of exertions involved in exercise routines (although, of course, unlocking your body smarts this way can be a valuable adjunct to an exercise or body-building program).

None of these physical IQ exercises take very long or tax you unduly. They are as much physical as mental. That's because it's your body's brain we are developing and educating, not your body itself.

DAY 15 ────────────────────────────

EXERCISE: TAPPING THE BODY'S WISDOM

This exercise puts you on the road to rapport with the deep wells of knowledge and wisdom stored within your physical intelligence. Self-made millionaires from the time of Andrew Carnegie right up to Donald Trump have attributed the investments and the acquisitions and mergers that made their fortunes to "gut instinct," a sudden intuitional sensation in the stomach that told then when and what to buy. Athletes who made a seemingly impossible play, or mothers who have lifted cars from their offspring's bodies with their bare hands, when asked what made them think they could succeed, inevitably say they "just knew" they could do it somehow. Top performers, in sports and the workplace, attribute their success to establishing perfect harmony with their body's instincts and just going with its flow, according to Charles Garfield and Hal Zina Bennett in their pioneering study, *Peak Performance.*

But for most of us, body smarts of this kind are a nearly unplumbed well of wisdom. However, today's exercise will lead you through a step-by-step process for getting in direct touch with your body's hidden wisdom.

THE POWER OF YOUR BODILY WISDOM

Getting in touch with your body may not sound as if it ought to be that difficult. After all, it's there, isn't it? All you have to do is check in with it, right?

If it were that cut and dried, you would already be rich in body smarts. Back on the African savannas millions of years ago our pred-ecessors were. They had to be. Since they didn't yet have words in which they could form their thoughts, they had to react to danger or the sight of succulent food entirely on the responses of their bodies.

You still have that kind of physical wisdom today. However, it remains bound tight most of the time, straightjacketed by cultural prohibitions and misunderstandings about the body. It emerges only in crisis or at unexpected moments. Yet getting in contact with your body smarts provides you (at the deepest physical level) with such profound sources of knowingness as gut feelings and other physical guidance, while enhancing performance, output, and productivity. Here is how the process works:

1. *Gut feelings and other physical guidance.* Gut feelings usually take the form of "good" versus "bad" sensations—a knotted stomach or a feeling of warmth and contentment. But the body also signals you via tension in the chest, headaches, sweaty palms, or a heart beating with anticipation. These kinds of "yes-no" messages have steered people away from unsound investments and unwise ventures and toward positive actions that have benefited their lives.

2. *Deeper levels of wisdom.* The body's innate intelligence can extend a surprising distance beyond simple yes-and-no answers, as the following story about human potentials coach Jean Houston, drawn from her book *The Possible Human*, indicates. At the age of twenty-three, Houston woke up one morning to find herself seriously ill. During the following nights her temperature would soar to 105 degrees, while by day "my name was Fatigue and I knew no other state." Doctors dismissed her condition as influenza and prescribed vitamins. One night she hallucinated a group of ladies in "flowered hats" who demanded Houston tell her mother to "give you the blood test that's given to alcoholics!" When she protested that she never drank more than a glass of wine a month, the ladies insisted they would keep pestering her all night, until she asked her mother for the test. Finally, Houston gave in, and to her surprise, her mother, a devout Christian Scientist normally opposed to medical procedures, instantly agreed to arrange for the test. The tests disclosed a rampant case of hepatitis, from which, properly diagnosed and treated, Houston duly recovered.

3. *Enhanced productivity.* That you can't work at your optimum if you aren't fully in touch with your body should go without saying. But most people plunge into the search for peak performance without ever pausing to consider their bodies at all. Yet even a little improvement in this all-important relationship leads to significantly greater output overall.

UNLOCKING THE THREE SHACKLES OF BODY SMARTS

If you're like many people, at this point you may be thinking something like, "If my body's so smart, then why does it take so long for me to learn anything?" Or "Then why is it taking me so long to correct that left hook?" Or "Why is it I can keyboard so flawlessly and fast some days and am a mistake-ridden klutz on others?"

The answer is simple. Almost from the moment we are born, those of us raised in Western culture are taught to see body and mind as two distinct entities that are often in conflict. This attitude, naturally, causes a split between mind and body, causing us to cut ourselves off from our physical intelligence, even to mistrust it. Science is rapidly overturning this view, which is based on a trio of misconceptions about the body. These misconceptions are:

1. The body is a dumb animal.
2. The body is bad.
3. Either way, it can't be trusted.

1. *The body is a dumb animal.* This view, derived from ancient misunderstandings about the way the mind works, saw the body as a lesser beast. In fact, it was often compared to a horse, which will inevitably make "dumb" mistakes or quit working and wander off course without the constant control of a rider (the conscious, reasoning mind) to keep it on track. The many times the body performed better, instinctively, without the intervention of the mind were seen as aberrations, not as abilities that anyone could repeat and learn.

2. *The body is bad.* This view stems from certain religious and early psychiatric traditions that the body's only impulses are toward gratifying pleasurable impulses—that if the body were given its way, all it would want was sex, food, and power. And in the absence of the superego, the soul or the conscious mind, the body would run amuck and do whatever it had to—including deceit, theft, and murder—in order to satisfy these needs. This view of the body (which is rejected by as many religions and schools of philosophy as accept it) overlooks the fact that the body is also the seat of our tenderest and most unselfish responses—from the way it knows how to embrace a child to communicate comfort and reassurance, to the instant response that sends a passing stranger dashing into a burning building to rescue a trapped tenant long before there is time to reason the matter through.

3. *Either way, it can't be trusted.* The body, dumb or evil? Take your pick. Both views put you at odds with your body. They mean that any time there is a conflict between your conscious mind and your body, you should always side with your mind and suppress the signals coming from your body, whether it's when to take a break or a gut feeling about a new client. Continuing studies of bodily IQ, however, point in the opposite direction: When it comes to the region of the physical, in a dispute between your mind and your body, give your body its head. Here, your physical-intelligence system will always know best.

The following exercise will unlock the fetters these three misconceptions place on your physical intelligence and will place the vast benefits of your body's wisdom at your fingertips.

PHYSICAL INTELLIGENCE BUILDER: TAPPING YOUR BODY'S WISDOM

Earlier in this book (page 22, in the section "The Five Mini-Exercises That Prove the Value of This Program"), you learned to identify your "signal" spot—the place in your body where your "gut" instincts typically manifest themselves (it isn't always in your belly). Now you are about to take a giant step forward. You will not only learn to tune-in on other signals your body is trying to send you, but to begin to read the wisdom they contain like a book.

To prepare yourself, locate a quiet spot where you won't be distracted.

1. *Sit or lie down in a comfortable position, and breathe deeply and slowly until you feel calm and relaxed.* (Throughout the remainder of the exercise continue breathing slowly and in a relaxed manner.)

2. *Focus your attention on your legs and feet.* (How do they feel? Are there any aches and pains? If so, ask yourself why you think this is? What are your legs and feet trying to tell you? Have you been standing on them too long, or perhaps not exercising enough? Or, do they feel fit and healthy? Are they signaling the sensation of well-being that follows a good workout?)

3. *Next, shift your attention to your arms and hands.* (What sensations do you detect there? Do your hands have a tendency to clench? What could your arms and hands be trying to tell you? Could there be someone or some thing you are angry at, but haven't, or can't easily, confront? Do your shoulder muscles have a tendency to tighten, as if hunching themselves against attack? Is there a problem you might be carrying on your back or expecting to soon fall on your shoulders? Or are your arms and hands relaxed and tingling? Are they sending a signal of satisfaction after a productive day's work?)

4. *Do the same with your torso.* (What is it telling you? A warm, peaceful sensation in your abdominal region might indicate your deep psyche, your inner self, senses all is well with the world around you. Tightness in the heart area could indicate unease or romantic concerns.)

5. *Finally, place your awareness in your neck and head.* (Again, ask yourself what the sensations there might be telling you. Tension in the neck could be the sign of your business partner, a real-life pain in the neck. A headache might be the analog of a headache-sized problem with the school building committee you're on.)

6. *Remain motionless for a few moments longer, and continue to take stock of your body.* Focus in on any new sensations you are experiencing, or any you might have missed before, always asking yourself what they might signify to you.

You need to do the entire exercise only a few times, until you find it relatively easy to identify and understand the signals your body sends. Then, once or twice each day, or during a crisis, you can simply "check in" with what your bodily wisdom is telling you. When you become accustomed to paying attention to messages from your physical intelligence, the answers to many of your most difficult dilemmas will become clear and you will gain a greater understanding of how you can best work in cooperation with it to boost productivity.

HOW THIS EXERCISE HELPED A TRIO OF CLIENTS ACHIEVE SUCCESS

Not long after beginning to practice this exercise, a client of mine, Lucille, phoned to say she had had been getting multiple signals from her body—headaches, tension in the shoulders, butterflies in the stomach—to buy her partner out of their medical practice. There were a few financial problems, and the two of them had been getting on each other's nerves lately. But Lucille felt loyal to her partner because they had done their internships together and started their practice together. Three months later, Lucille's partner skipped to Switzerland with all the money from the partnership accounts. Lucille swore that as far as she was concerned, this was the final validation of her body's wisdom, and she would pay greater heed to her gut feelings in the future.

Joseph used this technique to pace himself when his small insurance office fell on hard times, and he had to put in eighteen-hour days to turn the situation around. His body complained, of course, but Joseph just ignored it. After a couple of weeks of this regime, Joseph was in a state of permanent exhaustion, beginning to lose his edge as a salesman during the day and to make mistakes in his paperwork at night. Fewer hours were not an option, but by tuning in on his body, Joseph was able to tell when various muscles had been overworked and in need of a break and when his whole body needed a fifteen-minute breather. By working with his body's natural rhythms, rather than by fighting them, Joseph recouped his energy and was able to stay energized and alert throughout the entire six-month period.

It was also used by an NFL star and record-holding quarterback, whose name I am not at liberty to give, when he began to have difficulty with his celebrated long-distance pass. By listening carefully to his body wisdom, he was able to discover strained back muscles even his doctor had been unaware of, plus what he had been doing wrong to strain them. His career was quickly back on track, before his fans ever realized it might have been derailed.

THE SUPER BRAIN POWER TECHNIQUE YOU'LL LEARN TOMORROW

The second of the three days unlocks more of your body smarts with a potent exercise for learning any physical task quickly, easily, and, often, the first time through.

DAY 16 ————————————————————————————————
EXERCISE: WHOLE-BODY LEARNING

Today's physical-intelligence technique will come as a godsend to anyone who wants to be able to learn new skills almost instantly, or who typically has difficulty learning them. A facility for acquiring new abilities has been identified as essential to success in study after study. In that sense, this exercise alone will super-size your brain power and catapult you to the head of the class in any walk of life.

You can apply it to acquiring literally *any* office, athletic, professional, handicraft, recreational, or other form of bodily skill. The whole-body learning technique also makes a major contribution to performance speed, volume, and quality. As with the rest of the super brain power program, this exercise doesn't require you to develop some new ability. It simply shows you how to consciously access one you already have.

WHY YOU ARE ALREADY A SUPER-LEARNER

We are all super-learners—sometimes. Even if you are someone who dreads learning new physical abilities, think back over your life. You will find a time when you tackled a new jogging technique, or learned a new piece of music, or comprehended the sequence of keys needed to upload information on the company's new webpage template, or how to run an unfamiliar sewing machine, or how to pop a modem into a PC—instantly and effortlessly. Research suggests these kinds of experiences are universal, and almost everybody has had one.

Most of us dismiss such moments as flukes, especially as they do not repeat themselves. Until recently, science viewed such moments as flukes, too. Only in the past few years have studies begun to prove that this type of super-learning is an innate capacity we all share, and more important, it is one that can be trained and developed.

It doesn't matter if you are someone who "never gets it right," who sweats through every new learning challenge, who can't remember two things in a row, who needs to do something dozens of times before you even begin to get the hang of it. Deep within the brain, in the region of physical intelligence, you have all the hardwiring and software you need to become a super-learner.

The whole-body learning technique shows you how to make optimum use of your physical IQ. It unlocks another portion of your hidden genius, your "mental" body, by showing you how to make your physical and mental bodies work with, and not at cross-purposes to each other.

HOW YOU CAN DOUBLE YOUR LEARNING POWER

The reason we are such poor learners so much of the time is because we leave physical intelligence out of the equation. How can you learn to run that new combination fax, scanner, and high-quality color printer, or that three-ball combo shot in pool if you are doing it with only half your potential brain power? It's like swimming with one arm tied behind your back. You may just manage to stay afloat, but you aren't going to make very much progress in any particular direction.

It's a little-known fact, but you have two bodies: your physical body and a mental representation of your body in the region of the brain where your physical intelligence resides. It is this mental body that responds instinctively in emergencies, before your conscious mind is even aware anything has gone awry. Many human potentials experts call this "mental" body the "kinesthetic" body; martial artists often speak of it as "chi." The Egyptians apparently knew it as the "ka." It has been known for centuries, but was applied primarily to athletics and the martial arts, not to learning or productivity.

Ideally, your mental body and physical body are supposed to move and act in concert. But, without having been told to do otherwise, most of us override the urges and impulses of the mental body and consciously direct the physical body despite them, or at best, without being aware of them or taking them into account.

Seen this way, the explanation for our clumsiness, lack of coordination, and difficulty acquiring new physical skills is easily explained. It's like having one leg going one way and the other heading in a different direction. In fact, people even describe it as feeling exactly like that, when describing times they were particularly inept.

That's why it's like trying to learn with half your brain power tied behind your back. The following exercise is based on a simple principle: Get your physical body and mental body going in the same direction, at the same time, and you boost body smarts, physical memory, and productivity twice over. Is that a big enough step toward becoming a better learner to make the effort involved in trying this technique worthwhile?

SIX WAYS THIS EXERCISE MAKES YOU A SUPER-LEARNER AND SUPER-PRODUCER

I call this whole-body learning because, for the first time, you approach skill acquisition with your *whole* body, the physical and mental components, unified and working together. It may sound esoteric or like "psychobabble" at first. But it is based on simple neurological principles and has been used successfully by business people, athletes, and others to maximize both learning and performance. With it, you will be able to:

1. *Speed-learn physical skills, with almost zero mistakes.* Because your physical and mental bodies are working together rather than in different directions, you double your physical memory and learning abilities. You acquire new abilities faster and commit far fewer errors in the process.

2. *Increase performance, without increasing effort.* When your physical and mental bodies act in concord, you are more nimble and more quick, doing more and better work in less time.

3. *Prime the body to make the most of any physical task or learning experience.* By using this exercise as a "warm-up" that brings both your physical and mental bodies into harmony, you can be certain that you are at your learning optimum, so you can tackle any physical challenge with confidence.

4. *Reinforce learning afterward.* By sitting comfortably in a chair with your eyes closed, you can perform tasks over and over with your mental body until your get them right. (This is a variant of a technique known as "mental rehearsal.")

5. *Get out of your own way and let your body "do the walking."* Once you become accustomed to letting your physical and mental bodies work together this way, you will develop greater trust in your physical intelligence. When this happens, instead of getting in your own way by trying to control and second-guess your body (a job it can do better than you can), you will feel freer to let your body smarts take over and do the work for you, resulting in improved performance all around.

6. *Build stamina: work longer, absorb greater stress, resist illness better than others.* When physical and mental body act together, you have double the energy, double the endurance, and double the immunity to exhaustion, stress, and sickness.

PHYSICAL INTELLIGENCE BUILDER: WHOLE-BODY LEARNING

Find a place where there is room for you to stand and move your arms and legs comfortably in all directions. Stand in a natural, easy posture. Shut your eyes and begin to pay attention to your breathing for two or three minutes. This will help you both to relax and to focus your mind inward on your body. The first few times you may find this exercise a little awkward or that it is a bit of a stretch mentally. But stay the course and you will quickly get the hang of it. Plus, I think that like the majority of my clients, you will find it well repays the slight effort involved.

1. *Slowly raise your arms over your head and lower them,* paying equally careful attention to all the sensations of muscle, arm, flesh, and body this movement involves.

2. *Keep your arms at your sides, but imagine,* as vividly and in as much detail as you can, raising your arms over your head and lowering them (trying to actually feel the same sensations you experienced when you actually raised your arms).

3. *Alternate several times between lifting your physical arms and then your mental arms,* always attempting to feel the actions you perform with your mental body in the same detail you felt moving your physical body.

4. *Now raise your physical arms over your head.* Lower them slowly while simultaneously lifting your mental arms over your head. Then, reverse the process, lowering your mental arms to your sides, while raising your physical arms. Repeat until the sensations you feel in your mental arms are as intense as those from your physical arms.

5. *Lift your physical arms out from your sides in a "T" and rotate them clockwise in a circle.* Again, take notice of all the sensations your arms, shoulders, and neck experience. Then do the same with your mental arms, trying to feel the same sensations. Repeat both twice.

6. *Take a step to the right with your physical right leg and return, then do the same with your left leg.* Repeat with your mental legs, concentrating on feeling the same sensations. Repeat both twice each.

7. *Concentrate on feeling your physical arms as they hang at your sides.* Next, try to feel your mental arms occupying the same place as your physical arms. Now, try to simultaneously feel both your physical and mental arms at the same time.

8. *Raise your physical and mental arms simultaneously,* continuing to concentrate on being aware of both at the same time. Then lower them simultaneously, maintaining your focus on feeling them both. Repeat several times.

9. *Raise your physical and mental arms outward together in a "T" and begin to rotate them clockwise in concert.* Continue until you experience both physical and mental sensations with equal intensity.

10. *Step to the left and return, making the step with your physical and mental legs at the same moment.* Then do the same to the right. Continue, until you can feel your mental legs as a separate set of sensations moving in synchronization with your physical legs.

11. *Come to rest.* Draw in both a physical and mental breath. Feel both equally. Have your physical and mental lungs breathe slowly and evenly in concert until both your physical and mental bodies feel relaxed again and rested.

WHAT THE POWER-LEARNING TECHNIQUE CAN DO FOR YOU

As noted here, you can use this strategy to acquire literally any physical skill. The following examples are meant to show how two clients benefited from it.

Francine was the best tennis player among her large group of friends. She had begun to compete in tournaments locally, but although many of her opponents brought less focus to the game, Francine couldn't seem to develop the power and accuracy she needed to beat them. She had worked with a number of the best local tennis coaches, but still hadn't been able to acquire the strength and precision she was lacking.

When we talked, I realized Francine was playing with her physical body alone. Her mental body, and the physical IQ it could unlock, was left out of the equation. Using the whole-body learning technique, Francine got her physical and mental body working in synchronicity. Playing with all her body smarts, she began winning games with the power and precision she had been looking for.

Marcus had been an ace repairman for several years for a well-known company that manufactures and services postage meters. Then, zap, there was a cutback, and Marcus found himself looking for a new job. Since there aren't a preponderance of postage-meter companies, Marcus had to find similar work and finally secured employment repairing mechanical children's games for a famous pizza chain.

"Learning how to repair a different brand of postage meter wouldn't have been so hard," Marcus told me. "Or even one kind of game. But, they've got fifteen different kinds of games, not to mention a half-dozen variants with completely different works that you find in a few of the older franchises. I can't keep it all straight, and I'm thinking about quitting."

Marcus applied power-learning to his repair work. By performing the repairs with his physical and mental bodies working together, Marcus discovered he was remembering which repairs he made to which machines faster and that his fingers were picking up the skills almost on their own.

THE POWER TECHNIQUE YOU'LL LEARN TOMORROW

The final physical-intelligence exercise will give you the body smarts that allow super-salespeople like Zig Ziglar, world-class speakers like Tony Robbins, and all the great comedians and performers from Chaplin to Jim Carey, from Sinatra to Madonna, to instantly read where their audiences are emotionally and win their enthusiasm.

DAY 17 ─────────────────────────────────────
EXERCISE: INSTANT CONNECTING

Prepare to discover an unprecedented way of using your body as a key tool in achieving your goals. You are about to acquire a little-known skill that has carried many people to the heights of achieving their goals. People have gotten raises and promotions with it; bought companies and property with no money down; closed multimillion-dollar sales deals; won election to exclusive clubs; been elevated to partner; won unprecedented concessions from others; resolved disputes, impasses, and antagonism that stood in their path; and otherwise achieved success.

Yet this technique for super-sizing your brain power is so simple you don't even have to get up out of your chair. It shows you a method of using body smarts to gain the trust and cooperation of other people, settle disputes, and turn around the attitudes of even the most obdurate opponent. With it you can unlock more physical intelligence than you ever dreamed possible.

HOW YOUR BODY CAN DOUBLE YOUR CHANCES FOR SUCCESS

When most people think about the part the body plays in success, they pretty much limit their imagination to performance and productivity. But the body also affects your success in a much different, and equally important, way—and one that goes almost completely overlooked. Social scientists have found that your body is a key determinate in how people respond to you and whether they support your endeavors or undermine them.

In short, the body speaks volumes. Gestures, posture, expression are a language we can all instinctively read, and what we all instinctively respond to. As Charles Darwin, the great naturalist, has written, "God gave mankind facial expressions to show their intimate emotions." Experts agree: At least half of any conversation takes place between two bodies, not just between two people. And the nonverbal portion influences us just as much, if not more, than the verbal does.

Your nervousness about a new employee may be generated by his own stiff posture and edgy movements. Your crossed arms when being questioned about a downturn in your division's productivity might convey defensiveness to the new CEO. Or you may have gotten that grant because you were on a "high" the day of your interview, and your body language communicated your sense of self-confidence, ability, and intelligence particularly well. Or you might have cut short a business meeting when the prospect leaned far back in her chair, indicating she didn't want to have anything to do with your proposition.

Most discussions of body language focus on understanding it, so you can read the signals others send. This can provide invaluable insight into others, of course, but it is important to keep in mind that this is another of life's two-way streets. Body language isn't only something you can read; it is a medium through which you can communicate, as well.

There are times when projecting the right attitude is crucial to your success, such as during job interviews, while seeking a business loan at a bank, on entering a room full of unruly students as a substitute teacher, when presenting your idea for privatizing the school transportation system to the city council, or while asking out that good-looking clerk at the bookstore. In these and thousands of other daily interactions, the body language you use to communicate your feelings to others can literally make the difference between whether you go forward to a positive outcome or experience disappointment and failure.

With today's exercise, you will begin to consciously use body language to make a favorable impression whenever it's important. You will be able to turn those you meet into friends and allies, consistently securing a favorable response in the oh-so-important nonverbal 50 percent of your interactions with others. This one technique alone will advance you ahead of the field, at the very least doubling your odds for success.

HOW BODY SMARTS HELPED A FUND-RAISER CREATE TRUST AND SUPPORT

Sandi, a third-year college student in need of additional money for tuition, took a door-to-door job fund-raising for an environmental organization. As a trainee, Sandi spent her first day on the job following her supervisor around, watching him tell countless people what MassGreen was doing to save the wetlands and lobbing for a state-level Clean Water Act. People stopped to give him their time, attention, and money. Everywhere he went, Sandi's supervisor met with a surprisingly receptive response.

When Sandi's turn came, however, she was a dismal failure. For the first several hours, she went door-to-door as her supervisor had done in a similar neighborhood but her reception was a bit different. Even though she was given a neighborhood famed for its devotion to liberal causes and full of enthusiasm for MassGreen's cause, she kept coming up with a "big zero" on contributions.

Sandi went home that evening in tears and feeling completely confused. What had she done wrong that her supervisor had done right? He had said all the same things to similar people, yet when Sandi tried it, no one had wanted to listen.

The next day Sandi went out with her supervisor again and watched him work. She concentrated on trying to discover the difference between her approach and his. That difference, she found, was a unique form of body smarts. Simply by using his body to send one specific message over and over, her supervisor earned support and contributions from all those he contacted.

What Sandi discovered is a technique psychologists call "matching." Her supervisor consistently modified his own natural body language (posture, gestures, and speech patterns) to correspond to those of the person from whom he was seeking a contribution. If the other person was animated, he became animated; if the other person was deliberate and precise, he became deliberate and precise.

Though Sandy was unaware of the powerful psychological reasons this strategy worked so well (see the following), she decided to began applying it that afternoon, matching her own body language to that of prospective contributors. Soon she was performing as well as the other fund-raiser.

"MATCHING": FOUR STEPS TO INSTANT CONNECTION

Next time you watch a television-interview show, take a careful look at the physical actions and reactions of Larry King or Barbara Walters or Oprah Winfrey while they try to coax answers from their subject. You will notice that often the posture and attitude of the interviewer will closely match the body language of the celebrity they're interviewing. If the movie star or political leader or singer leans forward, then the interviewer will lean closer. If the celebrity becomes animated, the interviewer becomes animated, talking with his or her hands or picking up his or her coffee cup. If the person settles back in the chair and comes on low-key, the interviewer adopts a similar posture and attitude.

What's going on here? It's a simple technique the leading interviewers have all stumbled on, consciously or unconsciously, for instantly creating a positive emotional connection with their subject. So have all the most successful salespeople and politicians. It's the secret ingredient that makes their success possible.

It's "matching," a form of body language based on a simple, but critical, scientific finding. Studies show that the more like themselves someone is, the more people respond to and approve of that person. Matching establishes emotional rapport, gives them a sense of emotional safety, puts them at ease, makes them less defensive, and elicits trust, stimulates a desire to help you and agree with what you say.

Matching is yet another of those natural capacities you already have and draw on only haphazardly, but can learn to make fuller use of. Everyone unconsciously matches the body language of people around them without knowing it. Take a look around an office gathering sometime, and you will notice how often people lean forward when the boss does, or straighten when the boss straightens up.

Matching is easily observed in small groups of people who have spent a long time together and have gotten along well. If you have ever been married, or been in a long-term committed relationship, you probably noticed that both of you picked up mannerisms and pet phrases from each other. (This is the reason couples who have been together for many years start to "look alike." They have unconsciously begun to absorb and match each other's body language.)

In fact, from infancy on, much of our learning—and specifically our social learning—comes from matching. Babies are the perfect example: If you smile at them, they smile back; if you stare at them, they stare in return. For them, matching is a natural process, a way of learning about themselves and communicating with the world beyond. Matching plays a heavy role in adolescent peer groupings and, as we become young adults, in modeling correct workplace behaviors.

Studies reveal that the more in agreement two people are, the deeper the emotional connection they have made, the more their body language will correspond. They will lean toward each other, sigh at the same time, and have similar levels of energy. In most cases, they will conclude a mutually satisfactory deal or a conversation by nodding at each other, shaking hands with each other, or smiling or standing at the same time.

Conversely, the farther apart their views, the more people's body language differs. Scientists call this "mismatch." Research by business psychologists reveals that when two people interact, the outcome is negative in the vast majority (95 percent) of the cases where mismatch occurs. The parties involved either failed to come to agreement, reported negative opinions of each other, or described themselves as opposed to the other party's mission.

Research subjects who consciously "matched" their body language to that of another person, however, produced almost the opposite results. Matching created a feeling of connection in the other person and resulted in a positive outcome in a very high percentage of interactions (87 percent). Typical results included successful sales, job offers, expressions of goodwill, and promises of future support.

Researchers have confirmed that matching deepens the sense of emotional connection several ways. It helps you to:

- Consciously control the "unconscious" signals your body language sends others

- Win friends with body language that shows you and they share much in common

- Read other people's thoughts and moods at a glance

- Avoid sending any signals that undermine your efforts by suggesting you are angry, defensive, afraid, uninterested, restless, inattentive, or turned-off

Matching might seem artificial or manipulative at first, but it isn't. Matching is a natural human instinct that helps establish human connection. You are simply going to use it consciously to underscore that connection. Even if it feels awkward and self-conscious initially, keep with it and I believe you will find the bond it creates between you and others is so real, matching will soon become instinctive, like second nature to you.

As you grow proficient in this technique, you will discover other advantages, as well. Typically, people, like my student Christine, discover they acquire an unconscious facility for interpreting other's body language, reading people's moods and reactions at a glance. It's also common for people to report they have acquired a built-in truth detector. Christine told me she dumped one prospective suitor after the first date because his body language suggested he was lying to her about his job and background. Two weeks later she heard he had been arrested.

PHYSICAL INTELLIGENCE BUILDER: INSTANT CONNECTING

You are about to practice a highly focused variant of "matching" I call "instant connecting." You will find it a lifesaver when you need to build an immediate sense of rapport with another person. The exercise focuses on the four essential zones of body language: (1) head, eyes, and face, (2) arms and hands, (3) posture (upright, leaning forward or backward, slouched), and (4) general energy level.

1. Observe the four zones for the other person's body language.

2. Focus on the first zone: Is his expression serious, neutral, bored, eager, other? Where are his eyes focused, on you or somewhere else? Is his head erect, tilted to one side, or staring downward?

3. Focus on the second zone: Are his hands relaxed, clenched tight, fidgeting, waving in excitement? Do his arms hang naturally at his sides, or are they crossed defensively?

4. Focus on the third zone: What is his posture? Is he leaning toward you or away, slouched down or sitting erect and alert?

5. Focus on the fourth zone: Is he animated but scattered? Energetic but focused? Quiet and subdued?

6. Adapt your own body language to the other person's so that they match in each of the four zones. When the person cocks his head to one side while making a particularly important point, tilt your head when you are making one. If he holds his hands motionless in his lap, do likewise. If he sits erect when enthralled by something you say, sit erect when you want to show your interest in what he is saying. Whatever his energy level is, match it.

That's almost all there is to matching. However, a note of clarification is called for. Matching is not mimicking. There is an important difference. When people mimic someone, they literally copy the other's movements as that person is making them. In matching, you simulate their body language, not when they are using it, but later, at an appropriate place in the conversation, in the same kind of circumstances they would use it. (In short, if someone waves her hands in the air when she is talking excitedly, you don't wave your hands in the air when she waves hers. Instead, you gesture with yours when you are saying something you are excited about, too.)

It's probably wisest to practice first on a friend or family member who won't take offense if he or she does mistakenly think you are mimicking. If you do get caught, just laugh it off, tell the person about this book, and confess that you were practicing this exercise. You won't lose the friendship, and the person may be grateful for picking up a valuable new technique.

THE POWER TECHNIQUE YOU WILL LEARN TOMORROW

The final four days offer super brain power strategies for achieving success that develop the sixth key, your emotional genius. You'll acquire a sure touch for dealing with your own feelings and those of others in a positive, productive way that advances everyone toward his or her goals and establishes a firm foundation of support for your own success. Tomorrow's exercise details a method for unlocking, and using, the hidden genius of your emotions.

DAYS 18–21

The Sixth Key—

UNLOCKING YOUR EMOTIONAL GENIUS

WHAT'S YOUR
EMOTIONAL
IQ?

It's time to estimate the level of your emotional intelligence. Remember, the results are neither official nor scientific. If your score isn't what you would like, it means only that you haven't given your feeling smarts the exercise they need, and as a result aren't reaping their full benefit. After the four days of exercises that follow, your score on the following test should be twice as high or better.

Check the box beside any description that feels as if it applies to you. You

- ❐ Are empathetic, can easily sense what others feel, often from subtle physical clues, without having to be told.
- ❐ Are the kind of person friends, family, and colleagues seek out for advice and counsel.
- ❐ Enjoy group activities such as bridge, volleyball, or softball more than solitary ones such as jogging or swimming.
- ❐ Are tolerant of the faults and foibles of others.
- ❐ Are willing to ask others for their help and advice when you need it.
- ❐ Seldom lose your cool, blow your top, or fume when angry.
- ❐ Thrive under the challenge of teaching a person or group.
- ❐ Are considered a leader and mediator by others.
- ❐ Rarely are overwhelmed by bad moods, setbacks, and disappointments.

❐ Often develop your best ideas while talking to someone else.

❐ Feel comfortable around strangers, groups of new people, and crowds.

❐ Are socially active in volunteer organizations dedicated to the assistance of others.

❐ Are comfortable displaying affection with adults of either sex.

❐ Allow yourself to feel and express your emotions.

❐ Feel better once you have expressed and released painful or negative emotions.

❐ Infrequently become angry when someone takes a differing position, or even when attacked verbally.

❐ Take your feelings into account when making important decisions.

❐ Were popular in school, often involved in student government or other clubs.

❐ Work well with others and as a member of a team.

❐ Know what all the individuals of a group are feeling and are aware of the unspoken currents passing among them.

❐ Seldom waste time dwelling on past mistakes and failures.

❐ Rarely feel envious or jealous of others.

Scoring: Add up the number of boxes you checked.

If your score was between 1 and 5, you've let your emotional IQ go to seed. You may not like yourself very much. You may even have a somewhat negative view of life, react poorly to stress and adversity, let things get you down, and have few personal friends or allies at work. You may even feel emotionally walled off, uncomfortable with your own feelings and those of others. However, this section of the program is just what you need to breath the breathe life back into to your desiccated emotional intelligence.

If your score was between 6 and 12, you certainly don't hate yourself, and you have both friends and supportive colleagues. But adversity gets you down, you have moments of real unhappiness, and you are not at the head of your class in popularity—and probably not the leading candidate for advancement in your department, either (unless you are very good at what you do). Other people seem to have a knack for getting along that eludes you. Take heart, however. Days 18 to 21 will outfit you with the four basic techniques you need to get in touch with—and balance—your own emotions and those of others.

If your score was between 13 and 18, you get along with yourself and others well, are more positive than negative even in adversity, only occasionally experience real depression, and know that when others tell you they like you they mean it. In fact, your emotional intelligence is so high that with the help of the remaining four days of this program, you could easily go over the top and develop the kind of dynamic, magnetic personality that ensures you will achieve your dreams.

If your score was between 19 and 22, you are a charismatic, well-balanced individual, a popular person and a popular leader. You maintain a positive mental attitude, even when the going is at its roughest, and your emotional IQ is so near the top there is little or no room for improvement. You've probably made a career as an administrator, CEO, minister, marketing executive, politician, psychologist, teacher, or customer-service representative. Your world won't end if you skip the next four exercises, but I challenge you to give them a whirl and see if you still have the same appraisal of your emotional IQ afterward.

UNLOCKING YOUR EMOTIONAL INTELLIGENCE

These final four days bring the third week, and the super brain power program itself, to a close. You are about to master four skills that are necessities for those who would thrive in today's fast-paced, high-pressure workplace and for establishing the kinds of warm, caring feelings for others that are an essential of a successful personal life.

Emotional intelligence is the sixth key to your hidden genius. It encompasses every aspect of our interactions with others, from family and friends to managers, coworkers, and subordinates. Hoping to get anywhere in life without acquiring some measure of emotional intelligence is like attempting to steer a sailing ship *into* the wind. You can try with all your might to hold the course, but you can't hope to make much progress.

With these four emotional intelligence exercises, even if you scored low on the emotional IQ test (page 207), raising it is no hopeless task. (Which will be especially welcome news if you are someone who has always experienced difficulty with the emotional dimension in life.) If you can tell when you are feeling sad, angry, or joyful, the exercises for days 18 to 21 can show you how to super-size your emotional IQ in no time.

FOUR WAYS EMOTIONAL INTELLIGENCE MAKES YOU A WINNER

Emotional intelligence is nothing more complicated than being sensitive to your own feelings and those of others. People who are wise enough to exercise and raise their feeling smarts develop what Bruce Cryer, a human-performance consultant who works with Fortune 500 companies, calls "the four critical skills needed for personal leadership and emotional balance—self-awareness, emotional management, empathy, and positive relationships." These four skills, Cryer writes, give people "the deep personal and professional resiliency vital to preventing or overcoming hardships during this period of accelerated change."

If you think about the skills a manager, employee, CEO, politician, counselor, or just about anybody else needs to get through life, you understand why Cryer and others consider them so critical.

1. *Self-awareness.* This consists of being in touch with yourself, knowing what you feel when you feel it, and knowing that those feelings mean.

2. *Managing emotions.* This skill not only empowers you to put your own emotional responses in perspective and find positive ways to discharge negative feelings, it also allows you to tap deep emotional wellsprings that can supply the motivational fuel necessary to carry you through the rough spots when the going gets tough.

3. *Empathy.* This is nothing more than awareness of, and sensitivity to other people's feelings and perspectives.

4. *Positive relationships.* The all-important "social" skills that allow you to leave a warm, positive feeling with colleagues, family, and the person behind the supermarket counter, and which can carry you through the sometimes rocky seas of interpersonal relationships.

Those who raise their emotional IQs and develop these skills have a high "likability" factor, are gregarious, and get along well with others. They thrive by capitalizing on helpful feelings such as gut instincts. They know how to cultivate positive, beneficial emotions such as calmness, love, compassion, enthusiasm, and friendship, and they manage negative, destructive ones, such as anger, depression, and self-pity. On the job, at home, and while dealing with others in general, people with feeling smarts are adept at balancing honest expressions of emotion against respect, civility, and consideration. It's hardly any wonder they are usually first in line when personal plaudits and professional laurels are passed out.

HOW FEELINGS HELP KEEP INDIVIDUALS AND CORPORATIONS ON TRACK

Emotions might seem to have no legitimate role in the business world but, as a few moments' reflection will show, any individuals or organizations who leaves them out of the corporate equation are doomed to see success elude them and to have their goals remain unrealized dreams. For instance, dozens of companies have thrown out long-beloved packaging or advertising slogans in recent years, only to experience a sales slump when loyal consumers felt betrayed by the sudden change in an old familiar friend. On the other hand, marketing representatives with the kind of "emotional radar" that allows them to tune in to their clients' emotional concerns stand a very good chance of closing the sale. In the same vein, managers who raise their feeling smarts become more sensitive to their own emotions and those of staff members, which results in improved team harmony and enhances performance. And, employees who raise their own emotional IQs are seen as prime team players by managers and colleagues alike and can always rely on the support and cooperation of others.

In short, retiring at age forty with ten million dollars or returning to school at age forty to get that long-postponed doctorate are both equally impossible without better than average feeling smarts. Emotions are such a force to be reckoned with, says Maurice Elias, Ph.D., coauthor of *Promoting Social and Emotional Learning*, because they are our "warning systems as to what is really going on around us." Our feelings, Elias writes, "are our most reliable indicators of how things are in our lives. They are also like an internal gyroscope; emotions help keep us on the right track by making sure that we are led by more than cognition."

What's true for the individual, it turns out, is also true for the organization. Emotions, it seems, are the mental equivalent of physical pleasures and pains, psychological mechanisms that provide vital feedback—to both people and corporations—about whether something is good for them or when a decision has yielded less than desirable results. When things are going well, everyone tends to feel good. When they go poorly, feelings tend to shift toward the unpleasant. In this way, emotions act as feedback systems that help individuals and groups chart productive courses: To keep them going on the same track when things are going well and to signal to them the need to switch to another course when things are headed in the wrong direction.

WHY EMOTIONAL INTELLIGENCE CAN BUILD OR BANKRUPT A BUSINESS

In fact, due in part to Daniel Goleman's books popularizing the benefits of optimizing emotional intelligence, it has been proven to play an instrumental role in business success, so much so that four out of five American corporations now provide some form of training in feeling smarts, according to Cary Cherniss, a professor of psychology at Rutgers University. Cherniss found that American corporations spend over ten billion annually on programs that foster emotional IQ skills, resulting in improved customer service, leadership, and team-work.

One Chicago company, American Express Financial Advisors, began offering its employees emotional competence training when it realized its clients weren't buying life insurance, even when their financial plans clearly identified a need. A study revealed the problem: Life insurance is an emotionally charged subject for most individuals, and like most people, the American Express Financial Advisors' representatives had been taught to shut off their feelings in the workplace and were unable to switch them back on to order, so they continually failed to make the emotional connection with their client's concerns necessary to bring the deal to conclusion. At first, reports Kate Cannon, a company executive, when the emotional IQ sessions were introduced, "there were a lot of meetings where people rolled their eyes and had big smirks on their faces." But, Cannon says their smirks have turned into "grins of glee." As a result of the training they received, the sales force experienced sales increases up to 18 percent in some departments.

Roger Bailey, a psychologist and researcher, in his book *Leadership* tells the story of one mail-order jewelry catalog that experienced a sharp rise in profits after it learned the value of applying emotional intelligence to its business. The catalogue had produced consistent profits for many years, but new owners wanted to shake things up and stimulate growth. Roger Bailey investigated and found that the wide variety and freedom of choice the catalog prided itself on offering its customers was, rather than being an enticement to buy, a major deterrent to sales. People, it turns out, experience a certain amount of anxiety when they have to make choices. So the more choices they are offered, the more anxiety they feel before finally reaching a decision about what to purchase. The more anxiety people feel about spending money, the less willing they become about spending it, and so on. By taking this emotional factor into consideration and by simplifying the arrangement of its next catalog, the company realized the increased performance its new owners were seeking.

Organizations that ignore the lessons of emotional intelligence and put short-term profits ahead of building a solid foundation of employee and customer loyalty often pay a high price, according to Bailey. When one chain-store operation downsized hundred of employees at its outlets nationwide, the employees who remained lost all faith that the company valued them. Quality customer service—along with earnings—fell to an all-time low. The chain's customers quickly became dissatisfied with the quality of their shopping experience and voted with their feet, taking their business elsewhere.

TWELVE WAYS FEELING SMARTS CONTRIBUTE TO YOUR SUCCESS

They claim "things go better" with a certain famous soft drink. But I guarantee things really will go better on the home front, at the workplace, and everywhere between when you super-size your emotional IQ with the exercises in this final portion of the program. You will find the "slippery slope" to success becoming a fast track, because you have developed more than a dozen crucial success skills, including the ability to

- Tune in on what others are feeling at meetings, when being introduced to someone for the first time, with between lovers, during family discord

- Mesh smoothly with those at all organizational levels: teammates, colleagues, managers, support staff, customers, contractors, suppliers

- Become the kind of person others like instantly and want to help you achieve your goals.

- Establish the kind of instant rapport that creates sales, job offers, friendships, potential romantic partners

- Feel relaxed and comfortable with other people, whether it's one-on-one with strangers or a party crowded with people from a variety of social and ethnic backgrounds

- Become a leader who can get the things you need done by inspiring the enthusiasm and support of others

- Pour the oil on troubled waters that gets those two feuding team members to settle their differences in time to complete your project on schedule, or that brings your client and the prospective new vice president of regional production together despite their differences, or that resolves the decades-long bitterness between your sister and your mother

- Let your emotions be your guide; avoid that highly touted weekend workshop that turns out to be a disaster, green-light that new expansion everyone says isn't justified but that turns out to generate unheard-of revenue

- Identify and release toxic, negative emotions such as anger, jealousy, frustration, shame, envy

- Remain centered and upbeat; bounce back when the DOW dips by 500 points; when your master's thesis is turned down; when you are downsized out of a job; when you return home to find a spouse has moved out, leaving only a note

- Maintain your cool under pressure; when your positions are attacked or disputed at company meetings, family reunions, social gatherings

- Exercise the organizational, leadership, and communication skills that make you a top candidate for advancement

THREE PROVEN STRATEGIES FOR UNLOCKING YOUR EMOTIONAL IQ

Here are a trio of formulas for emotional well-being and personal success that should become lifelong bywords. Incorporate them into your daily life, and your feeling smarts as well as your own happiness will bear fruit and multiply.

1. To stay in touch with your own feelings, find time to write down your daily thoughts in a journal or computer file.

2. To inoculate yourself against worry and fatigue, bring enthusiasm to everything you do.

3. To discern the feelings behind other people's words and actions, ask yourself, "Why did that person they behave like that?" Attempt to "listen" with your eyes and "see" with your heart.

PUTTING THE POWER OF FEELING TO WORK FOR YOU

Days 18 and 19 show you ways of tuning on and developing the power of your own emotions as stepping stones to success. Days 20 and 21 offer proven strategies for forming strong, reciprocal relationships that provide you with the support you need to fulfill your personal and professional aims. When you complete them, this graduate-level course in super-sizing brain power will be over. You will have finished it in only twenty-one days. That's a modest investment considering it can yield a lifetime of success.

DAY 18 ————————————————————————————————

EXERCISE: PERSONAL RADAR

"Know thyself" isn't just some esoteric philosophic maxim. Instead, self-awareness is an essential quality of those who become successful. Self-awareness, says Kate Cannon, president of American Express Financial Advisors, is "about using the power of emotion to inform your thinking process. I think of it as working with everything you've got."

What is self-awareness? It is the ability to get in touch with your emotions, thoughts, actions, and reactions. It is knowing who, on a core level, you are, who you consider yourself to be, who you have been, and who you want to be.

We are born self-aware. No group is more in contact with its emotions than children. But as we grow older and listen to the prohibitions of our elders ("Don't cry, you're too old for that now"; "Keep it down, there's no need for so much excitement`") we moderate, lose touch with, or block off many of our feelings.

Today's self-awareness builder is a must if you are someone who is not as in touch with your emotions as you would like, or if you are someone who feels completely *out* of touch with your feelings. It will provide you with a direct line to your emotions. Self-awareness is so essential to realizing your dreams that you can release an astonishing reservoir of brain power with this one emotional IQ technique.

THE QUALITY BUSINESS LEADERS SHARE— AND HOW TO GET IT

Psychologist Robert Dilts, who interviewed dozens of business leaders, found each had an answer to three all-important, emotionally significant questions, "Who are you? What is your mission or goal in life? What are you feeling right now?"

If you don't know who you are, you can't expect to put yourself across to prospective employers, form solid relationships with coworkers, give fully to or get what you need from family members, or maintain your boundaries successfully in stressful or threatening situations. If you don't know what your mission or goal is, you can't expect to have fulfilling work, find the right friends and colleagues, or chart the course of your future life. If you don't know what you are feeling, how can you hope to respond well when asked for an opinion at a meeting, or you want to maintain a loving, romantic relationship with someone, or when your stress level is reaching dangerous proportions, or figure out why you suddenly snapped at your children this morning?

Can you answer all three of these questions? If you can, there's no doubt about the high level of *your* emotional intelligence. However, most people have trouble with one or another of these questions.

I call the technique showcased today "personal radar" because it empowers you to chart any areas of your inner emotional landscape that remain *terra incognita* to you. When you have completed it, you will be able to provide confident answers to the three preceding questions, or to any other emotionally charged area of your life.

The discoveries you make with personal radar enable you to

- Identify, explore, and release feelings for health and healing

- Find out what's truly important to you, so you can set your sights on getting it

- Tell whether you are compatible with jobs, colleagues, potential romantic partners

- Discover critical problems your rational, conscious mind is unaware of

- Be sensitive to negative emotions and the warnings they are trying to convey

- Be sensitive to positive feelings and the directions they are trying to guide you in

PERSONAL RADAR: SETTING THE FLIGHT PLAN FOR SUCCESS

Clearly, being in contact with your own emotions is as important to maintaining a fulfilling romantic relationship as it is to establishing positive relationships in the workplace. Otherwise, how can you know whether or not you are right for either?

When emotional factors are left out, the only basis for choosing a job becomes salary and security. Unfortunately, for all too many people these are the only factors they consider when seeking a position. Once they have secured a job, these individuals ignore or override any of their own emotions that don't make a comfortable match with their new employer's culture. Instead, they try to force themselves to fit into the company mold.

The consequences are rarely positive, as the nation's hospitals, psychotherapists' offices, and police blotters show. Stress, depression, addiction, and other acute psychological problems are so endemic that tens of millions take drugs such as Prozac to mitigate the symptoms. Tens of millions more are enrolled in various stress-reduction, depression-management, and recovery programs. Millions more attempt to tough it out alone, often losing careers, driving away loved ones, even losing control completely, and sometimes even taking their own lives and/or those of others in a headline-making fashion.

That's why, as an employee, self-awareness is so important. Can you answer the question: "Why did I choose this job?" Was it the amount of your weekly paycheck, or the challenge it offers you as an individual with your particular skills? Was it the fringe benefits, or the fun, stimulating office environment? Was it because of an ironclad seniority system, or the opportunity to grow and learn in your profession?

If your answers tend to fall into the first group of motives, rather than the second, there may be a serious disconnect between your current employment situation and your deeper emotional needs.

Those who work for companies such as Volvo Cars of Gent, Belgium, are less likely to experience stress and burnout and are more likely to report a sense of excitement and fulfillment about their work. What's Volvo's secret? An emphasis on four core qualities: employee satisfaction, quality environment, quality product, and shareholder satisfaction. Both companies and workers have a clear, conscious mission they can take pride in.

To put it in a nutshell: Self-awareness is the personal radar that can help you chart a flight plan toward personal and professional success and away from the storms and obstacles that loom across your path. You are more likely to achieve your dreams when you truly know who you are, what you want, and what you are feeling at every moment along the way. And if you lack that self-awareness, how can you expect anything except to find yourself in circumstances that fail to meet those needs, leaving you unhappy, depressed, even burned out?

No one has to stay permanently exiled from his or her feelings. Like an out-of-shape muscle, self-awareness can be exercised back into shape. Using the personal radar technique, the hidden genius of your emotional intelligence can easily be unlocked with a little effort.

HOW PERSONAL RADAR HELPED A SALES REP AVOID THE WRONG MOVE

Carlotta was an award-winning sales rep for a small-town branch office of a national term life insurance company. Her results were so impressive that the company offered her a better position with much greater earnings opportunities if she would transfer to her company's San Francisco office. The bigwigs at the San Francisco branch flew her out, wined and dined her, flattered her, introduced her to what seemed a congenial staff and an easygoing workplace.

When she flew back home, Carlotta's conscious mind had already decided that all the pluses were on the side of relocating to San Francisco. But when she arrived home, something about the move didn't feel right. Having taken one of my southern California classes, she used the personal radar exercise you will find following to explore her emotional reservations.

In the process, she discovered that though she liked the San Francisco staff, they just weren't as close and warm as the people in the small-town where she worked. She also realized that no amount of money could compensate for the small-town ambiance she loved so much. Letting her emotions be her guide, Carlotta turned down the San Francisco offer and stayed where she was.

The next year, she was a sales winner again. Would Carlotta have done as well if she had ignored her emotional intelligence and made the move to San Francisco? There is no way of knowing, of course, but if what we know about the role feelings play in success is any indication, the odds would seem to be against it.

EMOTIONAL INTELLIGENCE BUILDER: PERSONAL RADAR

The following three-step exercise will help heighten your self-awareness. It helps develop the personal radar needed to get in touch with the real you.

All that's required is a quiet room, a comfortable chair, paper and pencil, a computer file or a tape recorder. Sit down, stretch out, and take three or four deep relaxing breaths. Pick an object in the room, focus on it, concentrate hard, and block out everything else for two or three minutes. Then answer the following questions, each of which is designed to deepen self-awareness and put you in closer touch with your feeling smarts.

You will be answering three questions; take as much time as you need. Do each step in order; do not read ahead. You can write your answers or free-associate them into a tape recorder.

But don't leave out anything: moods and emotions, images, memories, smells. Whatever you feel, remember, or think, include it in your answer, no matter how insignificant it may see. Sometimes what appears trivial at first, or even a side issue, can direct you toward important feelings and key personal issues.

Even if you are someone who doesn't believe you feel much, or who feels walled off from your feelings, or even if you don't think you are feeling very much at first, give this exercise just a few minutes. As you begin to use personal radar to scan your inner emotional world, you will find one feeling or thought beginning to bring up another. And like the other super brain power techniques, with a little practice it will become almost automatic, and you won't need to formally sit down and work through the exercise to keep in touch with your feelings.

1. *Get in touch with what you feel bad about in life.* Finish the sentence, "What I feel bad about in my life is . . ." Don't leave out anything, the lack of privacy in your cubicle, someone who irritates you, the lack of parking near your office, people who always get your order wrong at fast food. (Here's what one workshop participant, Kelso, wrote, "I'm really not feeling bad about anything. Well, maybe a bit of frustration with the way they acted at the dry cleaners when they didn't have my shirts pressed on time. That really got my goat. They didn't have to be so demeaning. In fact, I'm boiling mad, and I'm not going to take my laundry there anymore. That's all. Otherwise, there isn't anything I feel bad about at all. Of course, my new boss does get under my skin from time to time. Our office was a really fun place to work before she came there. She is strictly a by-the-rules-type and is destroying our camaraderie and spontaneity. I really don't like her at all. She's making my job unbearable, and I am really beginning to hate her. Other than that there's nothing I feel bad about at all. I guess I am a little frustrated with the way my girlfriend suddenly announced she's flying off to visit her mother next weekend without any prior warning. I was planning for us to go to Big Bear for the skiing. Actually, I've been upset for a long time about the way she keeps making decisions, and committing herself to projects without consulting me.")

2. *Get in touch with what you feel good about in life.* Finish the sentence, "What I feel good about in my life is . . ." (List people and situations in your personal and private life, as well as strengths, talents, things you own that make you feel good, future plans, and so forth.) Again, try to be as detailed as possible. (Here's what Kelso wrote, "I like my work, I guess. I always wanted to work in graphic design. It's fun to see my work in magazines, on billboards, company reports, even television. I'm sure glad I didn't go into law, like my mother wanted. And I love the gang I parachute with every weekend. Nothing gives me a greater thrill. I know people don't think I'm enjoying myself all the time, but that's just because I'm reserved and have one of those faces that doesn't reveal what I'm feeling. But it's a real high. And I truly love Mary; she is not only the best lover I have ever had, but the most comfortable person I have ever lived with. I love her so much, I think it's time we started thinking about marriage. But I wonder if I show how I feel about her enough. Maybe I should work harder at that.")

3. *Learn and grow from what you feel.* Finish the sentence, "What I can learn from or do to improve the things I feel strongly about is . . ." Again, don't hesitate to be detailed. (Here's what Kelso wrote "I can see that I am not in very good touch with my feelings, because I always start off thinking I'm not feeling anything at all, and then I turn out to have some very strong feelings about a lot of things. I didn't realize I got so frustrated with my lover, and maybe I let that get in my way. But looking at things like this, I can truly see how much she means to me and that I could be putting in more effort to show it. There's clearly a problem brewing at my job, and I'm afraid I'm getting signals that it's time to begin looking for another one, one with a more congenial, artistic atmosphere.")

THE POWER TECHNIQUE YOU'LL LEARN TOMORROW

Now that you have learned how to identify your feelings with emotional radar, day 19 will present a technique you can use for developing the emotional confidence needed to deal with stress, setback, and opposition and to carry you through times when the motivational going gets tough.

DAY 19 ————————————————————————
EXERCISE: POWER CONFIDENCE

Day 18's exercise led you through discovering and interpreting your feelings. Today's technique shows you how to manage the negative ones by developing the kind of rock-solid confidence that in troubled times separates successes from failures. People who are confident that they can succeed tend to reach the finish line more often than those who are filled with doubts. Romeo was already confident he could win Juliet's love, or he would never have scaled her balcony in the first place. Lee Iacocca was already confident he could turn Chrysler around or he would never have left Ford to assume the helm of his near-bankrupt rival.

"You must believe that you can succeed, or you will evaporate in the corporate atmosphere. Being an executive demands extraordinary self-confidence from anybody. So before you consider embarking on an executive career, first examine yourself for any evidence of lagging self-confidence," says Marcille Gray Williams, who headed her own successful advertising firm at the age of twenty-three.

When the storm waters of difficulty, setback, opposition, or disaster break over some people, they meet it with unflappable assurance. Lacking that confidence, the rest of us succumb to such negative emotions as fear, anger, stress, panic, and, too often, they simply surrender. But beginning today you are going to build the feelings of confident self-assurance needed to manage the travails of private and professional life. This "power confidence" technique leads you one step at a time through a successful strategy for unlocking this vital portion of your hidden genius.

THE KEY TO AVOIDING STRESS, BURNOUT, AND DEFEAT

Life is a hotbed of emotions. In fact, human beings are the "most emotional animal," according to Donald Hebb, a Canadian psychologist. Hebb believes that as animals evolve and become more intelligent, they become more emotional. Rats are capable of fear; dogs experience fear, love, and jealousy; and chimpanzees have a range of emotions that seem almost human.

Though we supposedly become less emotional as we mature, Hebb is convinced that we become more emotional instead. Why don't we always seem that way? Hebb says, "We build human society so that we are carefully protected from our own emotional weaknesses, because we are so easily upset."

Family and romance have long been legendary generators of intense emotion. The pursuit of love, the feeling of love, the loss of love, even the betrayal of love produce some of the most acute feelings we can experience. Conflicts with parents, spouses, and siblings can generate almost overwhelming anger, hurt, frustration, and despair.

Even the most casual encounters of our day-to-day existence can generate intense emotion. A random interaction with a stranger can leave us feeling frustrated and furious, or, paradoxically, inspired and deeply touched. Friendships can make us secure, or they can irritate us to the point of exploding. Failing to carry the day with our proposal at the city-hall meeting can depress us for days. A spontaneous hug from our child leave us exhilarated, eager to share the story of the encounter with someone else.

But with the exception of a nod to the petty jealousies of office politics and the occasional steamy office affair, the workplace has traditionally been viewed as an environment from which feelings were to be excluded. This may have been some employers' ideal, but it is clearly a principle that has been honored more in the breach than in the observance.

Even on the face of it, few places would seem to be more ideally designed as ferments of intense emotion than the office place. All that's at stake there is our careers, hope of future advancement, prosperity, self-esteem, and professional standing. What better place to stir a whirlpool of emotional responses: joy, frustration, fury, triumph, failure?

In addition, there's the constant emotional stress of working hard, knowing every decision you make and every move you take is being evaluated from above. Except for those who can meet these pressures with unshakable confidence, two common emotional consequences are stress and burnout. Sadly, almost everyone today has experienced one or the other.

Chicago financial adviser Sharmayne Williams considers high emotional IQ essential to coping with the intense stress now that the stock market has become so "dicey." Once the pace would have sent her stress level soaring. "I could only marginally listen to what my clients were saying because I was so worried about how much I had to do." According to a *Newsweek* article, after training in the use of her emotional intelligence, Williams considers herself wiser about handling her feelings, "I've found that it takes twice as long to calm down from being stressed out than it does to stop it before it starts."

Like Sharmayne Williams, you can learn to use your feeling smarts to create the steadfast confidence that acts as a buffer against the negative emotions that create stress, burnout, or setback and "stop it before it starts." The following exercise does all this and goes an important step further. It shows you how to reignite the motivation necessary to getting back on your feet and in motion again, following setbacks or reverses.

The exercise guides you through a powerful strategy that enables you to face—and conquer—fear and other negative emotions that can shake your confidence. Research has shown that a key component of confidence is the knowledge that you are prepared for disaster and will survive it. This knowledge is what keeps the successes going till they have made their new business venture a go, obtained that dream job in the Bahamas, or received their Ph.D., and today's technique will show you how you can develop this indispensable aspect of your emotional IQ.

HOW TO DEVELOP A "NOTHING CAN SHAKE ME" ATTITUDE

Shawn was a nervous wreck. Though he had kicked the cigarette habit for more than twelve years, he was back to two smoking packs a day. There were deep lines grooved in his face, and his skin was loose and blotchy. His conversation was disconnected, repetitive, compulsive.

I hadn't seen Shawn in six years, but the last time we had met he had been a calm, assured young Silicon Valley software entrepreneur, and on the rise. Straight out of college, Shawn had started a company making encryption software to protect other software. The company had taken off almost instantly. Then followed five years of stratospheric growth. First it was a few employees and a small cinder-block building that once housed a dry cleaners. Then it was several dozen employees and an attractive redbrick building in an office park. Then it was several hundred employees and a new corporate head-quarters, designed to the company's specifications.

It was a lot of work for Shawn, long hours, few days off, almost no private life, mounting responsibilities. But, it was also so much fun, so exhilarating, that he hardly noticed how much work he was doing or just how far he was overextending himself physically and emotionally.

Then new, younger rivals with an even better encryption system showed up in the market, Shawn's sales curve began to flatten and even dip. From then on, one thing after another began to go wrong. Crises piled up, Shawn's hours became longer, the pressure mounted.

On top of his previous five years of extraordinary effort, the pace began to tell. Shawn started smoking again and began to see a thera-pist, but still he could feel himself "losing it." At times, he felt he was going crazy, at other times he was so depressed he felt paralyzed. He questioned every decision he made and lay up all night worrying, when he did get to bed.

Shawn was overwhelmed by anxiety, uncertainty, and the other typical feelings evoked by a confrontation with personal disaster and reversal. It was apparent that Shawn had no real confidence in him-self and so lacked the ability to bounce back from the many crises by which he was beset. In fact, Shawn had never really developed any confidence in himself. His early successes had all come easily, so he had never been in a position where this lack could become apparent. But once business reverses began to come his way, Shawn didn't have the kind of impenetrable faith in himself needed to weather and thrive during adversity.

I suggested this might be the source of his problem and told him about the power confidence exercise. But Shawn was too distracted to pay any attention. However, he e-mailed me a few days later and asked for a copy of the exercise, which I was happy to send him.

Later, through mutual friends I heard that Shawn used the "power confidence" exercise I taught him, and taken a new grip on himself and his company. Later, he developed a new breakthrough encryption program that was helping him recapture market share. I don't know for certain that he used the exercise; the timing could be coincidental. But the power confidence exercise has produced similar results for people like Shawn—and like you.

EMOTIONAL INTELLIGENCE BUILDER: POWER CONFIDENCE

The key to unshakable confidence, according to sports journalist and motivational speaker Alan Cutler, is the knowledge that you are prepared for the worst that can come, whether it's not getting that raise, losing your company, or starting over after the death of a spouse.

If you feel your confidence is in need of a boost, the exercise that follows takes you through a six-step process guaranteed to replace funk with fearlessness. You can use it to develop additional confidence, or when you are being overwhelmed by negative emotions following a catastrophe, or you need to generate some positive emotions for a critical motivational boast. Simply ask yourself:

1. *What specifically triggered the emotion?* Examining your anger, you may realize that being insulted by a clerk at a convenience store earlier in the day triggered it. Examining your stress, you may realize it began when your boss turned back the McGuffin report for extensive revisions, when you are already behind working on the Heinlein assignment. Examining your depression, you may realize it's because that new person in your social circle has been spreading malicious rumors about you.

2. *What's the worst possible outcome of the situation that triggered it?* Picture the worst result that you can imagine. In the case of the confrontation at the convenience store, you'd probably say it was that even if you did complain to the company that owned the store, they'd just blow you off, and you're just doomed to a life of putting up with petty insult and injury. In the case of your boss wanting revisions on one project while you are behind on another, you'd probably say it was about being fired, unable to find another job and ending up among the homeless living on the streets. In the case of the person disseminating malicious gossip, you'd probably say it was that you'd lose all your friends because they'd believe it.

3. *How would I deal with the pain if the worst did occur?* Whom would you turn to for emotional support? How would you deal with upset and loss of control? Whom could you rely on to help you work through the depression and self-criticism, and how could you ultimately forgive yourself for being human and imperfect? Perhaps you'd tell a sympathetic colleague about the clerk. Or you might turn to your parents, spouse, or lover for support if you lost your job. Or you might seek the comfort of your closest friend if everyone else you know turns against you.

4. *What would I do if the worst really did happen?* Suppose you complained and no one did anything about the clerk, and you were doomed to spend your life the butt of insults. . . . Or that you were fired and ended up on the street, homeless, begging for food, shivering in doorways or dangerous shelters at night. . . . Or that all your friends did drop you. . . . However bad the pain or humiliation or anger was at first, after the worst of the fallout had settled . . . Would you die? Would you kill yourself? Would you be ruined for life? Or would you just get back up on your feet and try again, just as you've done with all the other tough challenges you have faced during your life so far? (If the answer to the first two is, however grudgingly, a "no" and your answer, however grudgingly, to the last is a "yes," then you have already begun to find your confidence.)

5. *What can I do now to mitigate the effects if the worst does result?* Is there any possible way you could pick up the pieces if everything falls completely apart and get things back on track? (It may help to make a list of options.) If so, do it! Finally, are there options you have excluded because you don't consider them desirable or acceptable? What would have to happen for you to embrace those options as well? You might talk to a friend who is an attorney about your options if you complain to the owners of the convenience store and they refuse to discipline the clerk. You might begin to save more of your salary while putting feelers out among your friends and acquaintances for possible job openings in your field. Or you might ask your best friend to spread the word that there is another side to the story.

6. *What can I do now to increase the chances of a successful outcome?* Now that you no longer have to waste time worrying about the worst-case scenario (because you have a plan in place for coping with it), you are free to focus your energies on proactive strategies for forestalling it. What positive steps can you think of that you could take right now, today, that might prevent the worst from happening? You might bring a witness along the next time you visit the convenience store, when you complain, to substantiate your story. You might ask your boss for help or an extension on one of the overlapping projects and meanwhile decide to give up that weekend skiing trip. Or you might visit all your friends now and tell them the truth, and perhaps bring alone anyone who can back up your version and help dispel the rumors.

By now you may be noticing an enormous change in your emotions and mental attitude. Instead of being filled with worry and anxiety, you are probably feeling calmer and more confident, knowing that fate can do its worst and you will still bounce back and endure. Once you become adept at this process, you will find it begins to kick in automatically at the outset when anything goes wrong, allowing you to face the situation with assurance. Rather than wasting all the time and energy you typically lose to negative reactions, this approach allows you to get back to work immediately on turning the situation around.

THE POWER TECHNIQUE YOU WILL LEARN TOMORROW

To build solid relationships, you need empathy, the ability to sense, and identify with, the feelings of others. Other people are key factors in helping anyone achieve success, and knowing how to acknowledge and cope with their feelings is a must for personal or professional advancement. Tomorrow's super empathy exercise will raise your emotional IQ as far as tuning in on others' feelings and will more than double your interpersonal success power.

DAY 20 ━━━━━━━━━━━━━━━━━━━━━━━━━━━
EXERCISE: SUPER EMPATHY

On the previous nineteen days of this program, you have unlocked the powers of your six intelligences and developed dozens of super success skills. Now, it's time to take the final step and expand the portion of your emotional intelligence that encompasses the feelings of the other people in your life, for it is not possible to have a rewarding life or achieve lasting success unless you have warm, mutually supportive relationships with others.

That's why these two exercises have been placed at the end. They furnish the capstone to all that you have learned so far, by deepening your sensitivity to the others in your world and by giving you the tools to resolve differences when they crop up.

Today focuses on "empathy," a key emotional intelligence technique for establishing relationships with others. Empathy isn't anything complicated or difficult. It's simply the ability to identify with and understand "another's situation, feelings, and motives," according to my *American Heritage Dictionary of the English Language.*

Empathy is another of those super brain power skills that may not sound as if it ought to have that much to do with success but that, on deeper scrutiny, turns out to be a vital component. When my friend Haywood learned his fiancée's mother had suddenly been hospitalized, he didn't insist they proceed on their planned ski trip or fuss and fume because he was missing it. He understood what she must be feeling and insisted on spending the weekend at home by the telephone, where they could wait for news together. It certainly helped to cement his relationship with his girlfriend and her family.

When my friend Arlene noticed a certain amount of new reserve in her boss's manner, she uncovered a misunderstanding over her expense account that might have hurt her credibility had it been allowed to fester.

Marla, whom I met at a workshop, described how empathy had helped her make a difficult sale: She came to realize her prospect's resistance was based on long friendship and loyalty to the sales rep from a rival company. "Anyone could sympathize with that. I wouldn't want to injure any of my friends. And I told the client so. But there was one area where our product lines didn't overlap. So I asked the prospect if we could become his supplier in that one area, since it wouldn't cost his friend a single sale. He agreed. It was only small business at first, but three years later, when the prospect's friend retired, the fact that I had been so tactful won the same kind of loyalty for me, and he shifted all his business to us."

Drawing on advanced feeling smarts skills, today millions of sales and marketing people have developed "super empathy" using the same exercise for unlocking their hidden genius you will find following.

FIVE WAYS EMPATHY RAISES YOUR EMOTIONAL IQ

"If you wish to understand someone, first walk in their moccasins" is an ancient bit of Native American wisdom. But that's easier said than done. Exactly how do you go about "walking" in someone else's "moccasins" anyway?

The exercise that follows raises your emotional IQ by leading you step-by-step through a role-playing technique that literally places you inside the other person's head and allows you to see and respond to things—including yourself—the way they themselves see and respond to them.

Note: The following examples focus on conflicts with other people because, if you can learn to empathize with people who obstruct or slight you, then you can easily learn to empathize with anyone else. You can use empathy to tune in on someone in general, such as a new acquaintance or to understand why someone has resisted a business deal you want to close. Or you could use it to help you understand and share another's joy or sorrow.

In fact, this aspect of your feeling smarts raises your brain power by showing you how to

- Tune in on anyone's feelings, friends, coworkers, relatives

- Understand anyone's point of view, for successful negotiations, sales presentations, meetings

- Clarify what acquaintances, loved ones, or strangers meant when they acted the way they did, or said what they did, yesterday afternoon

- Figure out why a boss, teammate, or lover was in the mood he or she was in today

- Review for subtle emotional clues that tell when your interactions with others are on track and warn when they may be heading into an unproductive direction

EIGHT STEPS TO WALKING IN ANOTHER'S SHOES

In today's workplace, writes business consultant Patrick E. Merlevede, "empathy, the ability to put yourself in someone's shoes, as well as your capability of understanding someone's behavior are essential skills. A sales rep who is tuned in to a client's emotional concerns, for example, stands a better chance of making the sale. Managers who relate well to their staff get better results from those workers."

Anyone can learn to tune in to the emotions of other people in order to understand them better or grow closer. The key is putting yourself in the other person's shoes and then asking yourself the questions: "What do you feel?" "What do you see?" "What do you hear?"

The ability to do this is the secret of building genuine, long-lasting friendships. Based on shared feelings, these friendships not only enrich your life, but provide you with what performance gurus call having a "championship team" on your side, or your own "cheerleading section." Because you are in sympathy with them, they are in sympathy with you and provide you with a vital support network you can rely on in times of difficulty and distress.

Learning to understand someone else's feelings and see things from his or her point of view might sound like a formidable assignment, especially if you have never particularly exercised this part of your feeling smarts. But anyone can develop a flair for it by following these eight steps:

- Select a problem you are having with someone that has stirred emotions.

- Focus on exactly what triggered the emotions.

- Visualize the other person as she was at the time, and reflect for a moment on what you know about her.

- Picturing her in your mind, as if you were actually looking at her and having the same interaction right now, try to imagine the motive behind her action.

- Next, switch your perspective and imagine you are the other person and replay your own actions from her point of view.

- Evaluate how are you responding to yourself, now that you are standing in the other person's shoes.

- Look for a lesson you could apply to achieve a more positive outcome, or to give yourself a greater understanding and sympathy for the other person in the future.

- Finally, review: Are her motives and responses the same as, or different from, what you thought?

EMOTIONAL INTELLIGENCE BUILDER: SUPER EMPATHY

Before you begin, pick a time and place where you will be undisturbed for twenty minutes or so. Sit down, relax, and take three or four deep breaths. (Close your eyes if you feel comfortable doing that.)

1. *Select a problem that has stirred emotions you are having with someone.* It doesn't matter whether it's your emotions that were stirred or the other person's. (Though if the situation provoked feelings in one of you, it probably provoked them in both of you.) It could be a situation that has been plaguing you for a while, or it could be one that came up just today, for example, a colleague you keep locking horns with, or something rude someone said when your shopping cart accidentally nudged his at the supermarket.

2. *Focus on exactly what triggered the emotions.* If it's a colleague you are having a conflict with, it might be every time you propose a new venture at board meetings. If it's the person whom you banged baskets with at the supermarket, recall the exact words that made you angry or that hurt your feelings.

3. *Visualize the other person as he or she was at the time, and then reflect for a moment on what you know about the person.* If it's that business colleague, and you have known her for a while, this could include what she looks like and how she acts, where she went to school, random facts about her childhood, her current family relationships, ambitions, virtues, and shortcomings. If it's someone you encountered only once, for a few unpleasant moments at the supermarket, visualize him as you saw him at the time, his appearance, attitude, gestures, and body language.

4. *Picturing the other person in your mind,* as if you were actually looking at him or her and having the same interaction right now, try to imagine the motive behind his or her action. Ask yourself why your colleague always opposes you during board meetings or what motivated the person who was nasty to you at the market. (Often this step is enough to suggest the actions behind their feeling.) You may realize that your colleague always butts heads with you because she is concerned that every business decision have a rock-solid basis, whereas you believe that every company began as a risk someone took and that, unless a company continues to take risks occasionally, it can't survive and prosper. In the example of the unpleasant stranger at the supermarket, you might suspect that he had already had a bad day, or perhaps had an unhappy childhood.

5. *Next, switch your perspective;* imagine you are the other person and replay your own actions from his or her point of view. Picture yourself in his or her body, feeling what you imagine is what the person felt, with his or her background, looking out at you. See yourself, your gestures, your attitude. Perhaps there was what you intended as a confident smile on your face when that pesky colleague interrupted your suggestions with her penetrating questions? Perhaps you scowled when the person at the market began to chide you for bumping his cart.

6. *Evaluate how are you responding to yourself, now that you are standing in the other person's shoes.* Is there a difference? Might you see yourself as stubborn and bullheaded, or angrier than was called for? Perhaps your confident smile in the face of sincere questioning looks like a supercilious sneer and would have made you mad if you were on the receiving end. Or, perhaps, at the supermarket your scowl made it seem as if you didn't feel contrite and would become aggressive if asked politely for an apology, so you would have lashed out, too, if you were the other person.

7. *Look for a lesson you could apply to achieve a more positive outcome* or give yourself a greater understanding and sympathy for the other person in the future. From the fact that you and your colleague are both concerned about the company's best interests, but come at it from diametrically opposing philosophies, you might conclude that before presenting any risky proposition to the board, you will want to have as much solid evidence in your corner as possible, to minimize conflict. You might even decide to enlist your colleague in your endeavors, by asking her to help you search for the kind of support she finds convincing. And you might remember to check your smile when interrupted by her questions. As for the person at the supermarket, if your own words or manner played a contributing role, you may learn to manage them a bit better next time.

8. *Finally, review: Are their motives and responses the same as, or different from, what you thought?* In both cases they were, but your own attitude helped exacerbate the situation. Often this will be the outcome. But sometimes you will discover the other person's feelings were very different. (Your colleague might have been after your job, and this exercise might have revealed it.) Or you will discover you were right the first time. In the case of the person at the supermarket, your expression might have been conciliatory, and the other person's nastiness may have been all his fault. Your lesson might have been that while you can't change or prevent someone who's had a bad day (or life) from biting your head off from time to time, you can learn to shrug him or her off emotionally by realizing that, in the words of the late inspirational author Laura Huxley, "you are not the target."

THE POWER TECHNIQUE YOU'LL LEARN TOMORROW

On the final day of the super brain power program, you will discover the secret of achieving positive outcomes in all your emotional interactions with others, defusing conflict, hostility, and disagreements.

DAY 21 ———————————————————————
EXERCISE: CREATING POSITIVE OUTCOMES

On the final day of this three-week course you are about to learn the final step in achieving success: the secret of building long-lasting, mutually supportive relationships.

None of us operates in a vacuum. Other people always play an important role in our lives and in our careers.

You can't succeed in life without managing your relationships in a way that helps advance you toward your goals. Since other people have their own needs and aspirations, winning in today's world means creating outcomes that help the other person achieve their goals, while furthering your own—in short, solutions that ensure all the parties get what they want. This, in turn, creates the kinds of positive feelings toward one another that form the basis of enduring, supportive relationships.

"Modern entrepreneurs," writes emotional intelligence researcher Brian Van der Horst, "recognize the wisdom of working interdependently in order to be truly effective. The accelerating pace of change and the explosive proliferation of information has created a situation where no one person can possibly keep up without enlisting the support and help of others. In today's marketplace, you have to be skilled in negotiating the terms of interaction between yourself and your clients, colleagues or staff. Managing your relations is one of the competencies that are essential for emotional intelligence."

This last exercise shows you a staggeringly simple technique for arriving at a positive outcome, even in the most difficult and seemingly hopeless impasses or conflicts. Start using it today, and let the power of your hidden genius go to work building relationships and deepening friendships, weaving them into a safety net of well-wishers that will bear you up through any crisis.

SEVEN WAYS POSITIVE OUTCOMES BUILD YOUR SUCCESS

We all have interactions with other people every day. Monks sworn to silence leave their cells twice a day to congregate in the dining hall and silently consume their meals. Even the lonely cowboy (or girl) rides the range in pairs, in case a horse goes lame or there is some other rangeland disaster.

What we generally don't think about is that every encounter has an outcome. Every time we stop at a fast-food stand to grab a snack, or call up our internet provider to figure out why the program suddenly won't access our modem, or pass a coworker in the hall, or discuss the evening's meal plans with a roommate there is an outcome. It might be resolving a mix-up over our order quickly and pleasantly; it might be feeling dumb because the problem with the modem was so simple you should have thought of it yourself; or worrying that your colleague didn't smile; or it could be ending up with a delicious dinner you both will enjoy eating.

Typically, we become aware of outcomes only when we want something from an interaction, have a specific goal in mind, or find ourself in conflict with someone else and are having difficulty getting what we want. But all our interactions have outcomes, even if it is something as deceptively simple as a positive or negative feeling. These can range all the way from the trivial, like mild irritation or wondering how someone was feeling, to anger, humiliation, and resentment.

In fact, all interactions have three possible outcomes: negative, neutral, or positive. When we begin to look at our encounters with others this way and realize that each—however minor—*will* have a consequence, then we begin to become conscious of our interactions in a new way. We begin to make a conscious effort to do all that we can to ensure that each outcome is positive.

Positive encounters with others help create positive relationships in seven ways. They

- Generate goodwill
- Help get you what you want from the encounter
- Resolve tensions and differences
- Make others want to help further your endeavors
- Form the cornerstone of lasting relationships
- Create closeness and deepen friendships
- Provide a support network in emergencies and crises

When we are not conscious of promoting positive outcomes, the outcome of any encounter is left up to chance. At best, one out of three will produce a positive consequence. But two thirds of your outcomes will be negative or neutral. That's not a very good average, whether you are trying to get ahead in life or are merely in search of fulfilling relationships.

Encounters that leave negative outcomes

- Generate ill will and hostility
- Make it harder for you to get you want you want
- Generate tensions and differences
- Make others either indifferent to your aims or actively opposed
- Block the formation of relationships
- Create distance and injure friendships
- Leave you alone and isolated, with no one to turn to in emergencies and crises

WHY YOU WIN WHEN YOUR FOCUS IS HELPING THE OTHER PERSON WIN

How would you feel if you knew every person you had ever met had a sincere fondness and regard for you? Those who have mastered the art of creating positive outcomes face every day and every relationship secure in that knowledge. Clearly, it's in your interest to raise your emotional intelligence and consciously aim for positive outcomes in all your daily encounters.

Producing a positive outcome in every situation might seem like a pipe dream. How about, for instance, when you are arguing with your children over how you are apportioning your estate in your will? Or when you are deadlocked in a heated negotiation, where both sides feel aggrieved, and there is already some ill feeling as well as a wide difference in needs and objectives? Or when you and a lover both want two mutually irreconcilable things?

At one time, when an encounter led to conflict between two people, it was assumed one or the other would prevail, that, when it came to winning, in the words of the famous movie and television series, *Highlander,* "In the end, there can be only one." This was based on the apparently logical, but incorrect, belief that if there is a "winner" there must also be a "loser."

However, breakthroughs in such sciences as management theory, system dynamics, negotiation strategy, and outcome simulation have led to a radically new view of winning: When two people are in seeming conflict, no one has to be a loser. Both parties can leave the table winners.

You have probably heard of this approach. It's called "win-win," since everyone comes up winners, which is a lot like coming up roses.

The essence of this technique is that you give the other person the sense of being 100 percent in control of the situation, which, in turn, gives him or her a genuine emotional investment in making the final solution work. All it involves, is that you ask the *other person* to explain his or her needs, to propose the compromise or solution, to word any final agreement or conclusion you reach. The only part you play is making suggestions for how the other person might better include your own wants and views.

But because you have given the other person the power to choose an outcome that will have positive results for him or her, the person quickly becomes open to incorporating your wants and needs as well. Building positive relationships like this super-sizes brain power by adding to your own, the brain power of all those who regard you in a favorable light. You won't merely be doubling or trebling your hidden genius, you will be multiplying it by dozens or hundreds.

HOW POSITIVE OUTCOMES STRATEGY ENDED A CHAIRMAN AND CEO'S FEUD

Brian Van der Horst, former editor of *The Brain-Mind Bulletin* has been training French managers in competence in emotional intelligence for the last two decades. In one of his lectures, Van der Horst described an incident in which feeling smarts helped end a conflict between the chairman and CEO of an important French company. Van der Horst was called in when other management consultants, applying classic techniques for resolving issues problems such as power struggle and differing management styles, had failed.

With his expertise in intelligence, Van der Horst soon realized the problem was not differing management styles, but differing *thinking* styles. Both the chairman and CEO agreed on the company's mission. Both agreed on how the organization needed to evolve. But each had a different approach to getting there.

The chairman was most comfortable with gradual evolution. He wanted to institute changes one step at a time, which allowed for midcourse corrections before any policy could go disastrously wrong. He preferred to analyze and tackle problems one at a time, pinning down a solution for each before dealing with the next. The chairman valued the advice and input of others and always sought it before reaching a decision.

The CEO was most comfortable with rapid change. He felt morale was better and things went smoother when everything to be changed was changed all at the same time. He was comfortable juggling several balls at a time and preferred to leave his options open until the last possible moment, in case something altered the situation. The CEO had a strong sense of the value of his own judgment and preferred to reach final decisions on his own.

Van der Horst's solution involved coaching both the chairman and the CEO in emotional IQ techniques designed to create positive outcomes, even in seemingly irreconcilable conflicts. The two were then asked to revisit an issue that had long been a subject of disagreement between them. This strategy was designed to help people see past their surface differences to their underlying commonalities and then build on those commonalities to resolve their differences.

Working in harmony, the two former foes were able to devise a mutually agreeable strategy that combined rapid transformation of the workplace with controlled and continuous evolution. It was a win-win situation for both men. The outcome, which satisfied the deepest needs of both, resulted in a long period of expansion and growth for the company they led. Having learned to negotiate successful outcomes with each other, the chairman and CEO went on to become a famous corporate team in their own country.

When you raise your emotional IQ, as these two men did, it is possible to build bridges and produce positive outcomes, where both parties get what they want, across even those areas where the differences seem largest. The feeling smarts exercise that follows guides you step-by-step through a proven strategy for achieving positive outcomes every time and making every encounter a win-win situation.

EMOTIONAL INTELLIGENCE BUILDER: CREATING POSITIVE OUTCOMES

This technique provides you with an essential success skill. Its seven steps teach you the essentials of creating relationships and building friendships. (In the example used in the following exercise, you and your spouse are beginning to argue about how best to invest your savings. You want to take a significant portion and invest it directly in the stock market, especially in fast-growth stocks such as fiber optics. Your spouse insists that it all be kept in mutual funds and bonds.)

To begin, you will need the other person. Then follow these seven steps to create a positive outcome and leave positive feelings in your wake:

1. *Elicit the other person's thoughts, feelings, wants—not their position.* You probably know each other's positions, anyway; that's what you are fighting over. Instead, ask him/her to explain what makes the "why" behind the position or attitude he/she takes, the outcome he/she finds most desirable, and what would leave him/her with positive feelings. (Your spouse might reply that he/she has read too many stories about people who took their savings out of safe investments such as funds and bonds and put it in the market, only to lose it all when the market unexpectedly dipped and they couldn't meet their margin calls. Your spouse explains his/her father frittered away a lot of his money in commodities futures, and he/she doesn't want to end up dependent on social security as he did.)

2. *Share your own thoughts, feelings, wants—not your position.* Describe the outcome you find most desirable, what would leave you with positive feelings. (It might be eating you up inside that your money is earning only modest increases sitting in banks, funds, and bonds, where they won't do you any good until you are ready to retire. You want to have a substantial retirement account, but you saw your own parents postpone all their fun until their retirement, to ensure they'd have the savings to get them through—only they didn't live long enough to enjoy them. Meanwhile, you know, or have seen stories on the news about, people who are earning three and four times as much in the market and are able to take some out to enjoy now.)

3. *Focus on areas of agreement and commonality.* When you do, you often discover that you have more positions in common than in conflict. (For instance, you and your spouse both want to end up with money in the bank when you retire. You both want to keep a significant amount of your savings in safe investments. The only area of disagreement is how much to keep in banks, funds, and bonds.)

4. *Elicit the other person's ideas for a solution.* This takes away any defensiveness by giving him/her a feeling of being 100 percent in control of the outcome and having a 100 percent emotional investment in implementing the finalized version when you agree on one. (Your spouse, feeling in control, might surprise you by being secure enough to suggest that it would be okay for you to take 10 or 20 percent of the money earmarked for your retirement fund, and invest it in the market.)

5. *Ask if you could build on his/her thoughts and feelings by contributing a few of your own.* This gives the other person the opportunity to feel good about him/herself by being generous to you, which further increases his/her emotional investment in any developing solution. (If he/she offers 10 percent, you might suggest you could feel happier with the outcome if he/she could consider 15 or 20 percent.)

6. *Let the other person make the next suggestion* (repeating steps 4 and 5 until you have arrived at a satisfactory outcome in which you both have an emotional stake.) (Your spouse might suggest that in return for upping the percentage, he/she gets to pick some of the stocks or receives a veto over any investments you choose. If this is enough to make you happy, the negotiations might end there. Or they might continue until you have hashed out other vital details.)

7. *Make sure you have closure.* Ask the other person to restate your final solution as he/she understands it. If there are differences, you can catch them now. Plus, giving him/her the power to define or codify the agreement boosts his/her sense of control and emotional investment that much more. (Your spouse might frame the outcome as you understood it, or you might discover a misunderstanding over percentages or some other issue. But by always starting with the other person and asking for his/her idea of how to resolve the misunderstanding, his/her goodwill and sense of emotional involvement will make it easy to find an outcome satisfactory to you both.

Although the positive outcomes exercise is an unrivaled method for resolving disputes, the basic principles—always remembering that the other person has wants and goals, searching those out, and doing what you can to help them fulfill those aims—can be applied to even the most casual encounter. A harried clerk probably wants only a little kindness and patience from you, and these are not so difficult to provide. A roommate may want not only to resolve the dinner schedule, but to know his or her efforts on it are appreciated. Whatever the interaction, remember the positive outcome principles, and you will always leave warmth and goodwill behind, wherever you go.

THE POWER TECHNIQUE YOU WILL LEARN TOMORROW

Until they actually begin developing their six intelligences the way you have these last three weeks, most people are not aware of the potential brain power at their disposal. But once they experience the amazing benefits of their hidden genius in action, they realize a new world is opening to them. New methods of using their verbal, visual, logical, creative, physical, and emotional intelligences empower them to accomplish feats of thinking, remembering, learning, problem solving, and interacting with others.

But to fully unlock your hidden genius and unleash the miracles of your mind, you (and you alone) have the responsibility for continuing the program beyond this point. To reap its full benefits, you must determine to make tomorrow day 22 and continue applying these super brain power principles on your own in each of the days, weeks, months, and years that follow. I wish you good luck in doing so!

RECOMMENDED RESOURCES

Books

Abodaher, David. *Iacocca*. Macmillan, 1982.

Cooper, Robert K, Ph.D. *Executive EQ: Emotional Intelligence in Leadership and Organization*. Perigee, 1998.

Dilts, Robert, Ph.D. *Strategies of Genius*. Meta, 1995.

Elias, Maurice, Ph.D. *Emotionally Intelligent Parenting: How to Raise a Self-Disciplined, Responsible, Socially Skilled Child*. Three Rivers, 1999.

Elliot, Alan. *A Daily Dose of the American Dream*. Rutledge, 1998.

Finley, K. Thomas. *Mental Dynamics*. Prentice-Hall, 1991.

Funk, Wilfred. *Six Weeks to Words of Power*. Funk and Wagnalls, 1972.

Galloway, Tim. *The Inner World of Tennis*. Random House, 1974.

Gardner, Howard E. *Frames of Mind: The Theory of Multiple Intelligences*. Basic, 1993.

———. *Multiple Intelligences: The Theory in Practice*. Basic, 1993.

Garfield, Charles, Ph.D., and Hal Zina Bennet. *Peak Performance*. Houghton Mifflin, 1981.

Garfield, Patricia, Ph.D. *Creative Dreaming*. Fireside, 1995.

Girard, Joe. *Mastering Your Way to the Top*. Warner, 1995.

Goleman, Daniel, Ph.D. *Emotional Intelligence*. Bantam, 1997.

———. Ph.D. *Working with Emotional Intelligence*. Bantam, 1998.

Gross, Ronald. *Peak Learning.* St. Martin's, 1991.

Haggerty, Brian A. *Nurturing Intelligences: A Guide to Multiple Intelligences Theory and Teaching.* Addison-Wesley, 1995.

Harman, Willis, Ph.D., and Howard Rheingold. *Higher Creativity.* Tarcher, 1984.

Hendrie, Ph.D. *Emotional Intelligence at Work: The Untapped Edge for Success.* Jossey-Bass, 1997.

Hooper, Judith, and Dick Teresi. *The 3-Pound Universe.* Tarcher, 1991.

Huxley, Laura. *You Are Not the Target.* Wilshire, 1976.

Klinger, Eric, Ph.D. *Daydreaming.* Tarcher, 1990.

Lewis, David Lewis, and James Green. *Thinking Better.* Holt, 1982.

Lewis, Norman. *30 Days to a More Powerful Vocabulary.* Pocket, 1977.

McCarthy, Michael. *Mastering the Information Age.* Tarcher, 1991.

Minnelli, Vincente. *I Remember It Well.* Doubleday, 1974.

Olson, Robert. *The Art of Creative Thinking.* Perennial, 1986.

Robbins, Anthony. *Unlimited Power.* Ballantine, 1986.

Rossi, Ernest, Ph.D. *The 20 Minute Break: The New Science of Ultradian Rhythms.* Tarcher, 1989.

Simonton, Dean, Ph.D. *Genius, Creativity and Leadership.* Harvard University, 1984.

Stine, JeanMarie, and Camden Benares. *It's All in Your Head.* Prentice-Hall, 1992.

Stine, Jean Marie. *Double Your Brain Power.* Prentice-Hall, 1997.

Williams, Marcille Gray. *The New Executive Woman.* Chilton, 1977.

Witt, Scott. *How to Be Twice as Smart.* Parker, 1983.

Zey, Michael, Ph.D. *Winning with People.* St. Martin's, 1990.

Websites

Applied Neurolinguistics, 7 *Lessons In Emotional Intelligence Page*

URL:http://ourworld.compuserve.com/homepages/PatrickM/7eq_home.htm/

Brian Van der Horst *Home Page*

URL:http://ourworld.compuserve.com/homepages/brianvanderhorst/

Educational Systems Design *Howard Gardner Page*

URL: www.ed.psu.edu/insys/ESD/Gardner/menu.html/

Edweb's *The Theory of Multiple Intelligence Page*

URL: http://edweb.gsn.org/edref.mi.intro.html/

Emotionally Intelligent Parenting *Home Page*

URL: http:.//www.eqparenting.com/

Give 6 Seconds for Emotional Intelligence *Home Page*

URL: http://www.6seconds.org/index.shtml

Improving the Classroom Through Multiple Intelligences *Home Page*

URL: www.scrtec.org/wizard/pages/02202.html/

James Manketlow's *Mindtools Home Page*

URL: www.mindtools.com/

Teaching to the Seven Multiple Intelligences

URL: www.iols.com/users/berolart/GRPWEBPG.HTM/

Theater in Motion's *Multiple Intelligence Resources Page*

URL: www.theatreinmotion.com/resources/

INDEX

INDEX

W